Leading to Empower

Biblical Perspectives on the Art of Leading and Managing People

BY

Michael Jelliffe

Nenge Books, Australia

Leading to Empower

Biblical Perspectives on the Art of Leading and Managing People

Copyright © 2020 Michael A. Jelliffe
All rights reserved.

Without limiting rights under the copyright above, no part of this publication shall be reproduced, stored in or introduced into a retrieval system, or transmitted in any form or by any means (electronic, mechanical, photocopy, recording or otherwise), without the prior written permission of the publisher and author of this book.

Published by Nenge Books, Australia, March 2020
nengebooks1@gmail.com
Design by Nenge Books.
Cover photo - Morning in Waigani suburb, Port Moresby. Copyright © 2020 Michael A. Jelliffe.

Scripture quotations taken from The Holy Bible, New International Version® NIV®
Copyright © 1973 1978 1984 2011 by Biblica, Inc. TM
Used by permission. All rights reserved worldwide.

Nenge Books publishes quality ebooks and hardcopy books using print-on-demand technology to provide cost effective results for small and large print runs. For author enquiries or to order this book, email to nengebooks1@gmail.com

Also available as an ebook ISBN 978-0-6488206-0-4

ISBN 978-0-6484284-9-7

> Now that I, your Lord and Teacher, have washed your feet, you should also wash one another's feet. I have set you an example that you should do as I have done for you.
>
> John 13:14-15 (NIV)

CONTENTS

Foreword	6
Preface	7
Introduction	9
1. God the Manager	**11**
1.1 God has a Vision - Genesis 1:26	13
1.2 God is Creative - Genesis 1:27	15
1.3 God establishes Boundaries & Rules - Gen 1:28	16
1.4 God provides Resources - Gen 1:29,30	17
1.5 God Reviews - Genesis 1:31a	18
1.6 God gains Satisfaction - Genesis 1:31	19
1.7 God Rested - Genesis 2:2	20
Summary	22
QUESTIONS FOR DISCUSSION	23
2. The Heart of Leadership - Wisdom	**24**
The Wisdom of Solomon	26
QUESTIONS FOR DISCUSSION	30
3. Empowering People	**31**
3.1 Use what the team has	36
3.2 Give them authority	36
3.3 Make failures learning experiences	37
QUESTIONS FOR DISCUSSION	38
4. Servant Leadership	**39**
Washing the disciples feet	41
The Marks of a Servant Leader	42

QUESTIONS FOR DISCUSSION	44
5. Communication and Listening	**45**
God's Communication Strategy	49
Listening	51
QUESTIONS FOR DISCUSSION	53
6. Resolving Conflict	**54**
Paul and Barnabas	57
Principles for conflict resolution	59
Summary	61
QUESTIONS FOR DISCUSSION	62
7. Managing Job Peformance	**63**
Measuring Performance	68
Performance Gaps	70
Performance Management	72
QUESTIONS FOR DISCUSSION	76
8. Delegation	**77**
QUESTIONS FOR DISCUSSION	82
9. Mentoring	**83**
QUESTIONS FOR DISCUSSION	89
10. Values Driven Management	**90**
QUESTIONS FOR DISCUSSION	95
Case Studies in conflict resolution	96
Performance Management Simulations	100
About the Author	105

Foreword

It is my privilege to write this foreword to Michael Jelliffe's book *Leading to Empower*.

This book records principles that have been his passion for the training and development of men and women over many years. I have been connected with Mike for nearly 40 years. Our lives have been linked with Mike and his wife Kathy because of our common understanding of God's calling to a missional commitment. Whether it be through provision from our work or from the church, God has graciously enabled us to serve Him, both in our own countries and overseas with people of other cultures.

A study of Scripture shows that in development of our vocation, God brings together our job skills and Biblical skills. I am impressed how Mike brings together both parts of this developmental process. Mike's use of the Scriptures highlights both work related and Bible related principles in the empowerment of leaders. He has identified these common experiences that God uses to grow leaders through examples and case studies drawn from his own encounters in the workplace.

The principles and skills outlined in this small book will be of help to both younger and senior people. We need more people who sense God's calling to an increasing responsibility to transfer these principles, characteristics and skills in the development of a new generation of empowered leadership. I commend this book for use as a personal manual and a training text for the workplace.

Kevin White
MA ICS, Reg.Elect.Insp, Dip AET, Cert ALE(voc)
Technical Training Development Manager

PREFACE

The Bible as a text book on management?

Besides its value in terms of historical, geographical, cultural, ethnic, archaeological, spiritual and other information, the Bible gives us many insights into working with people and the art of leadership and people management.

This book attempts to look at some of those principles, recognising that they provide a foundation for developing the most effective people management skills, whether in business, public service, NGO, club, church or at home. At the heart of good leadership is the ability to empower people. The leaders who can manage people from the paradigm of empowerment will revolutionise their relationship with their team, with much better results in productivity, morale and team well-being.

Coming out of my own management experiences and material I have developed in teaching frontline management courses, I hope this book inspires you to consider the Bible in a new light, one that illuminates its wisdom in an area some may have not considered before. But leading and empowering people is really at the heart of what God's mission in the world is about, isn't it?

Management ideas and principles are not new. My aim has been to draw out people empowerment principles from Biblical text and frame them in the context of practical management practice.

I acknowledge Kris Cole and her book, *SUPERVISION, The Theory and Practice of First-Line Management* (2nd ed., Pearson Education Australia, 2001) as a primary reference text. She distils so many ideas and concepts as well as practical applications and I have benefited from those. Kevin White's contribution of source material in Chapter 8 as well as participation in seminars and as a friend and mentor is similarly acknowledged. Readers may be aware of theirs and others' footprints like watermarks on some pages as they read. I have appreciated their contributions to empowering leadership.

Finally I'd like to thank the many people, particularly in Papua New Guinea, who I have been privileged to work with or teach and who have helped me understand the value of empowerment better.

My passion is to see people empowered and be able to achieve all that they are capable of, reaching all of their God given potential. I hope this book is a help in empowering you as a leader or manager to achieve your potential in that role.

Michael Jelliffe
March 2020

Introduction

Any learning is only valuable to the extent that it is applied. This book is designed for use by individuals but also for small or class groups as a learning resource. It can be used, for example, during a weekly staff meeting over 10 weeks, one chapter a week.

Each chapter begins with a simple case study, a practical example of a situation relevant to that topic. At the end of each chapter are some questions to prompt discussion, which group leaders can use to prompt practical application of that topic in context.

Case studies and simulation exercises at the end of the book are also a good way to think about how the principles can be applied in the real world. Case studies can be read out to the group who then provide feedback in a group discussion. Simulation exercises are always a lot of fun. Select two people to participate but do not allow them to see the other person's role description. Give them a few minutes to read over their role and explain it further if necessary before allowing them to act out their role. I find it also useful to keep the rest of the group, who are observers, unaware of what the roles are so they can provide genuine feedback on what they saw. Why not write your own case studies and role plays based on situations in your work experience?

Please email me at nengebooks1@gmail.com with any feedback.

Michael Jelliffe

1. God the Manager

Rosie was very excited when she was asked by the General Manager to take up a role as a departmental manager in the organisation. She had worked there for five years and knew all the systems well. In fact, everyone said she was recommended for the position because she knew how everything worked and could get things done.

But six months later she was discouraged and frustrated.

"I thought I knew what being a manager was all about," she confided to her best friend, Jeni, as they sat in the company cafeteria at morning tea. "But I can't seem to get anything happening and I'm not meeting the department's goals, we're getting more and more behind. I'm scared the boss will sack me soon!"

Jeni listened to her friend and then began to ask her some questions.

"Have you been working harder and longer hours now you are a manager?"

"Oh yes, definitely," responded Rosie, "I'm here well after normal knock off time, and often take work home to do. I'm at it seven days a week."

"Have you had to take on more work then?" asked Jeni.

"Oh man, you wouldn't believe how much extra is involved in being a manager. It seems I not only have my own work but have to do half of my staff's jobs as well."

Jeni listened to her friend as she responded to a few more questions and then said,

Leading to Empower

"Rosie, I think I know what your problem is."

"Well I'm at the end of my rope if I'm honest, so if you can help me, I'll be very grateful to you," said Rosie. "What's my problem?"

Jeni paused for a moment, thinking how she could best phrase her answer.

"I don't think you understand what management is about," she said gently to Rosie. "You seem to relate management to the amount of work you do and the amount of time it takes you. You are focused on trying to get a certain amount of work done, your own and your staff's. But there is a different model of management which I'd like to share with you."

"Isn't that what management is all about though, making sure that you achieve the work that your department has to do? How can there be a different kind of management?" Rosie asked.

"You are partly correct Rosie, but management is all about working with people to achieve the outcomes, the work package if you like, that is needed. Your focus on tasks is distracting you from a focus on empowering your staff. I think that the best ways of understanding people management that works are found in the Bible. So can I share with you some Biblical principles which will help you understand a better way for you to manage?" asked Jeni.

"Well if you really think these will help me, yes, I'd love to hear these, can you start now?" replied Rosie.

In her mind she also recognised that her husband, Barry, was struggling with his management role and for the last three years, since he had been in a senior management position, he had come home almost every night frustrated and stressed by his work. "It should be easy," he would say, "I know what needs to be done but at the end of the month we are always behind schedule, and the guys in my department are always grizzling about something." Rosie wondered if Jeni's advice would be good for Barry as well.

"Let's start at the beginning of the Bible then," suggested Jeni, "in the book of Genesis, chapter 1. We'll establish first of all what a manager is," said Jeni, as she led into the discussion with Rosie.

In Genesis chapter 1 there is a basic outline of a management cycle which really sets the stage for us in understanding effective, empowering, people management. After creating the heavens, earth and animal kingdom, the final act of God's creation as recorded in the book of Genesis was the creation of mankind. We'll start reading the story at Genesis chapter 1, vs 26 and see the seven principles of management that God initiated.

1.1 God has a Vision - Genesis 1:26

In looking out over the heavens, world and animal kingdom as created thus far in Genesis, it seems that God knew something was still missing. None of the things created so far had the capacity to enter into a personal relationship with God, yet that was God's vision and heart's desire - to create people who would be in a relationship with Him.

So God speaks out this vision of mankind, *"let us make man..."*, created *"in our image, in our likeness"*, and with authority to rule over all of the world God had created - fish of the sea, birds of the air, livestock over all the earth, and all creatures on the ground.

This is a sweeping vision of God's intent, the visionary plan for the final stage of creation - people who were made with a capacity unique in the created kingdom to relate to God their Creator, who contained some element or elements of similarity with God that nothing else in the created world contained.

Every step forward to achieve something new must commence with a vision. Not all managers are visionaries, but those who exercise clear people leadership skills start with a vision. While personality profiling may help some people identify if their tendency is more to visionary leadership than bureaucratic pen pushing, a vision of what is to be achieved must be at the heart of every organisation and project, large or small, if it is to succeed. The vision may be something shared by a group of people or from one person, but key to its success is the ability of a leader to speak out that vision, to articulate it, to share it and pull others into it as they are inspired by it.

Most organisations these days have a Vision Statement which heads up their organisational advertising. It is important that managers and leaders keep this vision in the forefront of their people's minds, constantly reminding them of WHY the organisation exists. While a vision statement may look like a slogan, it needs to set out clearly what the organisation seeks to achieve rather than just be a catch phrase. When people embrace a vision rather than a set of rules or procedures, they begin to own what it means, and their participation in the organisation becomes something they feel at a heart level and commit themselves to. Otherwise other agendas take over and their participation in the organisation become focused on what they can get from the organisation rather than what they can give to it.

> ### Reflection
>
> From what you know of the Bible stories and life of Jesus, what would you say was his vision?
>
> Can you express that in a statement?
>
> How did Jesus pull in key people to that vision?

1.2 God is Creative - Genesis 1:27

Very simply stated, God now creates man and woman, fulfilling the first part of the vision. The next chapter of Genesis, chapter 2, contains a more graphic picture of this creation sequence, stating that God made man *"from the dust of the ground"* in verse 7. Whatever the mechanics of this miraculous event, one element is clear - God created this first man from nothing but dust. In other words God made something amazing out of next to nothing.

To be able to 'make something out of nothing' is probably a fair description of how a leader or manager must be able to act at times. Situations frequently arise when you are managing people where a high level of creativity is required. The wise leader is able to manufacture a solution which enables a win-win solution, empowering all those concerned, when it all may have seemed hopeless. Creativity is an essential skill for leaders and people managers.

> **Reflection**
>
> Can you think of a story in the Bible where a leader exercised creativity in solving a problem or finding a solution to a challenge?

1.3 God establishes Boundaries and Rules - Genesis 1:28

God now establishes the rules by which mankind can exercise authority on earth, effectively giving them their job description. Mankind is instructed to populate the earth and have authority over the animal kingdom. In Genesis 2:15-17 God further expands on this by setting specific limitations or boundaries for mankind, stating that they would work the land and care for it, establishing an environmental agenda, while prohibiting eating of the fruit from one tree, the 'tree of the knowledge of good and evil'.

Every organisation has its rules, policies and practices. Without these people will have no idea of what their part is and how they are to play that part in the organisation. These will include "no go" areas, limits or boundaries which members should not enter into. Often these are enshrined in a Code of Conduct which includes behaviours as well as actions that are unacceptable for members of that group. For churches, the Bible is in itself a Code of Conduct document, though there are numerous interpretations which mean that not all churches may agree to the same meaning of each text. But the 10 Commandments in themselves are a very basic Code of Conduct that is adhered to by nearly all people around the world regardless of religion. The exception of course is those who are so radicalised in their religion, ideology or cultural practices that they consider that killing an enemy, abusing people or fraud is acceptable.

A good leader not only advises people of the relevant code, but inspires people to uphold it by their own lifestyle.

God also sets out the consequence of busting the boundary - 'eat of that fruit and you shall die'. People at all levels of organisation, whether it be government, private enterprise, not-for-profit, volunteer or church based, should be very clear about what the standard of behaviour of that organisation is, and what the consequence of breaching that standard are.

> **Reflection**
>
> Can you think of any examples in Bible stories of someone busting the acceptable code and suffering consequences, and also of a leader upholding the code, maintaining the boundaries that God set?

1.4 God provides Resources - Genesis 1:29,30

A good people manager not only assigns people their tasks but under-girds that by ensuring they are adequately resourced to carry out the assignment. So God provides the nutritional resources to mankind, allocating every seed-bearing plant and every tree that has fruit with seed in it as food. Once again we have an expansion of this in Genesis 2 where a prohibition on one tree was given. In a similar gesture, God allocates every green plant as food for the animal kingdom.

Providing resources for those carrying out a task is in fact a primary role for any manager. A leader who does not empower their team members to be able to carry out their task is more likely hindering the team's ability to successfully meet their job goals, and reach the vision. Sustenance is important, for any task must be sustained right through to completion if it is to be successful. To resource empowerment means more than just supplying raw materials and tools to do the job, it means ensuring the team members are motivated and working together, being encouraged and rewarded.

> **Reflection**
>
> What examples are there of Biblical leaders empowering their people with resources to do what is required?

1.5 God Reviews - Genesis 1:31a

As God reviewed all that had been created, he came to a conclusion, that it *'was good'*. The review process is essential to being able to determine whether a job has been done well or not. These days we talk of Performance Indicators and targets. I wonder how God would have expressed Performance Indicators for mankind's creation?

Setting targets and reviewing a job are a primary way of answering the questions:

- have we achieved the vision?
- what sort of standard have we achieved?
- how do I know if I have done a good job or can do better?

So reviewing a team's work against established criteria is an integral part of a manager's role.

> **Reflection**
>
> Do you think Jesus had the equivalent of performance targets for his ministry on earth?
>
> What did he want to achieve?
>
> Did he achieve it?
>
> Did Jesus have performance targets for his disciples?
>
> Is there any example of Jesus reviewing the disciple's success in ministry?

1.6 God gains Satisfaction - Genesis 1:31

God seems to have gained immense pleasure and joy when he looked back over the creation and all that he had achieved in the past six days. God's summary was *'it was very good'*.

The work of managing should be very satisfying. When a job is done well, to the manager's satisfaction, it creates a deep sense of well-being and achievement, in other words, a real sense of motivation for both manager and team members.

Leading people can be very frustrating, especially when you feel like people are actually not willing or not wanting to follow you. But when you are successful in leading others and in achieving the goals of a project together, the rewards in terms of personal motivation are huge. This motivation empowers you to continue in your leadership as well as teaching you what you did right that you can apply to your next team project.

> **Reflection**
>
> Can you think of a team project that you managed that gave you real satisfaction - what was it that resulted in gaining that satisfaction, or dissatisfaction, if that was the case?

1.7 God Rested - Genesis 2:2

Here is the critical last step that most managers fail to follow, with the resultant exhaustion, burn out, physical and emotional distress, loss of vision, loss of leadership ability, loss of motivation, to name a few. The Biblical emphasis on one day in seven as a rest day should not be ignored. While it may not be practical for everyone to set aside every seventh day as a rest day, churches follow this principle in marking one day a week for church services and fellowship. I always think it is a pity that for pastors and lay ministers, this day is actually the busiest of the week for them! So it is important for them to manage their time well so that they find their rest day during the week.

In a survey of many aspects of management that I conduct in management training courses, the issue that most people raise as needing improvement is time management - learning to manage their own time well. Setting aside adequate time for rest and using self-management strategies are critical for any manager who wishes to not only survive but also excel in their role of empowering others.

> **Reflection**
>
> In what ways did Jesus practice gaining rest time?
>
> How hard is it for you to get regular rest time?

SUMMARY

1. So we see that a manager is someone who has a **vision** for what needs to happen, they understand exactly what they need to achieve, whether that is their own goal or handed to them by their boss.
2. They also have a **creative** ability, call it initiative, to see how to make things happen, sometimes out of next to nothing.
3. They are able to set **boundaries** about what needs to happen, recognising what behaviour will help and what behaviour will not help.
4. Their focus is on empowering their team to achieve together and so they provide the necessary **resources** for their team members so they can be at their most productive, and most motivated.
5. When the team completes the job they spend time **reviewing**, seeing how well their team performed, with the specific goal of empowering them to do better.
6. When the team has done a good job and they are satisfied, the manager is also **satisfied**. The manager knows that job satisfaction for his or her staff is the most important single issue to doing a good job.
7. And when its all done, the manager throws a bbq, or gives them an additional day off to **rest**.

Notice that the manager's job is not to do all the work for the team. The manager's job is to make sure the work gets done, by providing visionary leadership, resourcing, reviewing and creatively trouble shooting to see that the team members reach their potential and are successful.

Leading to Empower

QUESTIONS FOR DISCUSSION

1. How was Rosie's understanding of being a manager hindering her from gaining job satisfaction?

2. Until now, what has been your understanding of what a manager does?

3. Review the 7 phases of management above. What aspects of the manager's role are new to you?

4. Which of these 7 phases are you actively doing in your management role?

5. Which of these 7 phases are you not doing? How can you start to include these aspects in your own management role?

6. Does your organisation embrace this kind of approach to management or does it follow another model of management?

7. What can you do to help your organisation move more to this kind of people empowering management?

2. The Heart of Leadership – Wisdom

When Kila started working in the company eight years ago, he knew what he wanted right from the start.

"By the time I'm 30 years old, I'll be the most influential person in this industry. I will be charging big money for consultations because people will know that I am very successful and know how to make money quickly," he bragged to his wife soon after they were married.

She was soon to realise how committed he was to this vision and raised her eyebrows in surprise. He'd quickly worked his way up the corporate ladder to a senior management position where he was brokering deals worth millions for the company, earning good money and starting to make a name for himself in the industry.

The knock on the front door of their house one day surprised her, especially when she answered to a detective police officer. But surprise turned to shock when he told her that Kila had been arrested and was in prison awaiting court.

Apparently he had been involved in a scam for a couple of years where he was doing some underhand deals, secretly selling off company assets and banking the money in a separate personal account.

"It's easy for young men seeking fame and fortune to make unwise choices," the detective told Kila's wife. Her shock quickly turned to sadness for her husband. Tomorrow was his 30th birthday.

The corporate world usually sets very high goals for employees and managers to achieve through and for their organisation. These goals set the standards by which employees will work within the company. Managers strive to achieve these standards and improve on them. Success is seen in terms of how well employees and the company in general achieve these goals (which are usually financial targets, especially in public companies).

Behind these goals are two values: to be successful in both financial and personal spheres. These two values are seen to be at the heart of everything the company and employees, especially managers, seek to do. A successful manager is seen as one who has risen up the management ladder to where he or she is now earning a good wage and receiving lots of benefits, including housing, vehicle and bonus payments. Financial success of the company will take the manager down the path to personal success through increased responsibility and a better contract. At the same time, financial success at a personal level is also seen as the mark of a good manager, someone who has made the grade.

Many people seem to accept that these goals are the most important drivers of how they function at work, and so everything for them is focused on achieving better recognition (fame) and the best financial package possible (fortune).

The Bible seems to question this viewpoint of the corporate world. In fact, it tells us quite clearly that fame and fortune are not the pathway to success. Much more often they are the road to failure.

The Wisdom of Solomon

In 1 Kings 3 we read the amazing story of King Solomon. The second son of King David and Bathsheba, Solomon was anointed to the throne of Israel by his father, David. The story and intrigue of these events precede chapter 3. Solomon conducted a massive capital building project which included walls around Jerusalem, a palace and an awe inspiring temple laced with gold. God appeared to him in a dream, and said, *"Ask for whatever you want me to give you."* I Kings 3:5 (NIV)

Despite his upbringing as the King's son, where he would no doubt have been tutored by the best scholars in Israel and lived a life of luxury, Solomon was humbled by the huge task of leading the nation of Israel. He acknowledges that he is only in this position now because of God's kindness to his father, David, and now to himself. He laments:

"Now O Lord my God, you have made your servant king in place of my father David. But I am only a little child and do not know how to carry out my duties. Your servant is here among the people you have chosen, a great people, too numerous to count or number. So give your servant a discerning heart to govern your people and to distinguish between right and wrong. For who is able to govern this great people of yours?" I Kings 3:7-9 (NIV)

The burden of leadership rested heavily on Solomon's shoulders. To be managing huge infrastructure projects, creating alliances with rival nations, and dealing with the fall out from his dysfunctional family did not hide his innermost feelings of dependence on God, or his lack of confidence in his own ability. So his humble request was for Godly wisdom, the ability to discern what is really happening behind the scenes, so that his judgements will reflect what God seeks for his people.

God's reply is straight forward.

"Since you have asked for this and not long life or wealth for yourself, nor have asked for the death of your enemies but for discernment in administering justice, I will do what you ask. I will give you a wise and discerning heart, so that there will never have been anyone like you, nor will there ever be. Moreover, I will give you what you have not asked for - both riches and honour - so that in your lifetime you will have no equal among kings." I Kings 3:11-13 (NIV)

Fortune and fame, riches and honour. How often are they what we seek? But as Solomon humbled himself before God and sought wisdom, God, in acknowledgement of Solomon's humility and need, graciously promises to give him fame and fortune as well.

Solomon went on to write several books in the Old Testament, including Proverbs, Ecclesiastes and Song of Songs, known as the wisdom literature of the Bible. Each of these books exhorts us to set wisdom as the baseline of our lifestyle. Here are some examples from Proverbs:

"The fear of the Lord is the beginning of knowledge,
   but fools despise wisdom and discipline."

Proverbs 1:7 (NIV)

"For the Lord gives wisdom,
   and from his mouth come knowledge and understanding,
He holds victory in store for the upright,
   he is a shield to those whose walk is blameless,
for he guards the course of the just
   and protects the way of the faithful ones.
Then you will understand what is right and just and fair -
   every good path,

For wisdom will enter your heart,
*   and knowledge will be pleasant to your soul.*
Discretion will protect you ,
*   and understanding will guard you.*
Wisdom will save you from the ways of wicked men..."

Proverbs 2:6-12 (NIV)

"Wisdom is more precious than rubies,
*   and nothing you desire can compare with her."*

Proverbs 8:11 (NIV)

Wisdom is core to leadership and management, but what is it? Wisdom incorporates a number of aspects which the Psalms allude to - having a depth of **understanding** of a situation so that when you speak, your words reflect that knowledge. In other words, you know what you are talking about. Wisdom gives you **discretion**, so you are smart about the circumstances relevant to making a decision. You understand that there are **short term and long term affects** from this decision. You understand the **background context** but also the long term **implications**, how this might affect people or situations in the future. You are aware of the **interests of the people involved** and discern when there are **hidden motives** behind people's intentions.

But most of all, you understand that there is a **God** who sees every person and situation. So when you place yourself and your decision making in this framework of a higher power at work, you place yourself in an ethical and moral framework, seeking to ensure that your decisions are *right and just and fair*. To do this, your own ethics and morality are challenged to make sure that your motives are good and not compromising ethical standards, either your own personal standards, your organisation's, or God's. That is wisdom.

Too often wisdom is sacrificed at the corporate alter of fame and fortune. Too many achieve fame and fortune but if it is not the result of wise choices, it will come crumbling down quickly. Corruption and nepotism are traps that leaders too easily fall into in their desire for fame and fortune. Wisdom keeps the manager focusing on justice, honouring discretion, loving honesty and integrity, and maintaining self-discipline. Leading with Godly wisdom is a heart matter, it raises us above the worldly values which seek personal fame and fortune, and enables us to respect that there is a greater power at work in the world whose values we need to adhere to if we are to achieve true success.

James speaks about two kinds of wisdom when he asks,

"Who is wise and understanding among you? Let him show it by his good life, by deeds done in the humility that comes from wisdom. But if you harbour bitter envy and selfish ambition in your hearts, do not boast about it or deny the truth. Such 'wisdom' does not come down from heaven but is earthly, unspiritual, of the devil. For where you have envy and selfish ambition, there you find disorder and every evil practice." James 3:13-16 (NIV)

How many leaders and managers have fallen into this trap of selfish ambition, engaging in unethical or evil practices which are contrary to God's values? As a result they have found their workplace and family life in chaos and disorder, and themselves in court.

This great contrast between wisdom and selfish ambition highlights a key principle in successful leadership, and that is the principle of empowering others. True leadership is not about pushing yourself up the corporate ladder so that you can achieve success through fame and fortune. That is selfishness, which empowers personal greed. No, true leadership is about empowering others to achieve their

God-given potential as people created by God. It is about being available for others. The wisdom that God equips us with as leaders and managers is to be able to discern the most effective means of empowering those who are under our sphere of influence. That is the vision that Solomon saw and desired so much - how he could successfully lead God's nation of Israel to achieve all that God had for them.

QUESTIONS FOR DISCUSSION

1. Kila may have been smart in being able to make money, but was he wise?

2. What do you think is the dominant value in your organisation - fame and fortune, or wisdom?

3. What is your own personal dominant value?

4. How can poor choices undermine an organisation's ability to manage its people well?

5. What can you do to seek to make wisdom more central to your management and leadership style?

3. EMPOWERING PEOPLE

Some years ago I was approached to conduct a consultancy in a large corporation in Sydney. Their workforce was very multicultural with most of the workers involved in manufacturing complex electronic equipment. The management team had become very frustrated because they could not move forward with bringing changes to staff benefits, such as uniforms, because the union had created a climate of mistrust between staff and management. There was also the issue of language and cultural diversity making it harder to communicate meaningfully in English. They had lost days and days of productivity time trying to negotiate with employees, and still had no result. My brief was to find out what the staff wanted in regard to the staff benefits and conditions being promoted by management. I recognised there were two challenges - the low English levels in the multicultural workforce, and the negative attitudes towards management.

I set about to familiarise myself with the staff environment while meeting them all at work. I did this by spending several hours just walking around the workbenches introducing myself and finding out what each person did in their work role. I also sought to see what they thought might be their preferences in the issues involved. I wanted to establish a rapport with as many of the staff as possible before moving to the next step, but also gain some appreciation of what they saw as the solutions to the issues.

I decided to use a game as a tool to gauge staff preferences. So I created a card game which had a number of possible choices for each issue written on cards. These reflected the answers they had given me earlier at the workbenches. This also provided a more visual approach to the choices possible which made it easier for those with low English literacy to understand.

Once I had made up and assembled all the cards, I called out workers in small groups to meet for one hour, and we played the game in a room dedicated by management for me to use. I tried to make the environment as relaxed as possible, and of course, the workers had already met me at their workbench so I was familiar to them. As we discussed each issue, I invited the workers to select the card which reflected their feelings or preferences best, and place that on the game board. At the end of all the sessions, I had a group of cards that I tallied up which provided data on staff preferences.

When I presented this in a report to the manager, just two weeks after commencing the project, he was very surprised, pleasantly so. "We've wasted weeks of man-hours trying to get this result with no success, and you have done it with only one man-hour per person wasted!"

So why did I have such success when management could not? The union had created such distrust of management that the negative reactions to anything management may have proposed, even if it was in the best interest of the workers, meant that management could not bridge that gap of negativity. There was no relationship on which to build trust. Even though I was contracted by management, I came as an independent person and so was able to bypass that negativity by creating my own positive relationship with the workers. Even with just a few minutes with some of the workers at their workbenches was enough to start to build a bridge of trust with them. There were some who were sceptical of management doing anything but I was able to get cooperation from most of the workers.

Secondly, I believe that the mechanism of the card game enabled workers to make a choice secretly and express their opinion in a way which freed them from having to conform to the outside pressure from either the union or management. They could make their own choice independently, without complex English *language issues causing misunderstanding or ambiguity, just as they watched their colleagues select cards and do the same. These choices were in fact made up of the same ones they had already expressed to me when visiting their workbenches. So this process was not management trying to decide for them, it was them deciding on their own choices, something I made very clear as we played the game. This was empowering them, giving them their own voice, and I believe that made the difference.*

※

While **management** is about organisation and policies and processes to achieve specified outcomes, usually technically related to the goals of the organisation, **leadership** is about how that is achieved through working with the people in the organisation. The two are related in that effective leadership will inspire and motivate people to achieve more and do a better job, which in turn will reflect positively at a management level, such as greater success in achieving organisational performance goals.

There are a number of models of leadership that are recognisable but one that is very common is the **authoritarian** approach. In this model, the leader/manager bases their relationships with others on their job position and the organisational authority inherent in that management position. In this model, managers see themselves as the boss. They are in charge and make the decisions, and their team is there to do what they want. Success is based on how well the team follows their instructions. Otherwise they face disciplinary action, if not the manager's anger, if they do things any other way or fail to deliver the outcomes desired. Managers like this will often demand that other staff must do what they are telling them because of their authority as the manager. They feel that their ascribed position of authority means the team is there to do what they want, and when. Incompetence, insubordination or failure to meet job expectations are seen as issues which need to be dealt with by disciplinary measures.

The main problem with this model is that it doesn't work very well. Why? Because it makes people feel intimidated and devalues their worth. In some cases workers can be quite scared of their boss, and living on tenderhooks wondering if they might be demoted or lose their job at any time. The relationship between manager and staff becomes one of toleration, based on trying to keep the boss happy, while knowing that the boss is never going to be happy! The result is that the worker is demotivated and will never achieve their best in their work situation. A team of workers feeling this way will never effectively contribute productively to achieving performance targets and helping their organisation grow. Their focus is on surviving their job and doing whatever they can to try and keep the boss happy, not on excelling at their job.

The opposite of the authoritarian model of leadership is one that seeks to empower team members rather than control them. The **empowering model of leadership**, which we will deal with more in the next chapter on servant leadership, recognises that the greatest potential to achieve is found in allowing motivated people to flourish, experiment, think and work together in creative and inspiring relationships. Therefore the *relationship* between the manager and the team becomes the most important element, not the *work* to be done.

To function at this level requires no less authority but it is authority that is earned, not assigned. Earned authority is based on respect, not job position, and therefore is primarily relational rather than hierarchical.

Akio Morita, Chair of Sony and author of "Made in Japan" is quoted as saying:

"The most successful leader in business is not the man who goes around giving detailed instructions to his subordinates. It is the man who gives his subordinates only general guidelines and instils confidence in them and helps them do good work." [1]

> # LEADERSHIP IS NOT ABOUT MAKING PEOPLE WORK. IT'S ABOUT LETTING PEOPLE WORK
> Lee Doricott

No one better demonstrates this empowering model of leadership than Jesus. In the Gospels we read the story of his earthly life and ministry. He drew in his twelve main disciples as well as a growing number of others, including women, who travelled with him. What made them drop everything and follow him after only a few words, "Come, follow me."? How did he keep this band of followers for three years living with little or no home comforts, no salary or benefits, roaming around poor communities? His ability to motivate them was amazing.

While Jesus taught his disciples many things, he also looked for ways to allow them to put his teachings into practice. Their three years with him was in fact an apprenticeship in learning life and ministry. Whenever the opportunity arose, Jesus allowed them to experience first hand what he was teaching them to do. This was how Jesus planned to change the world through 12 men!

---

[1]. Both quotes are quoted in *Supervision - the Theory and Practice of First-Line Management* by Kris Cole, 2001, Prentice Hall, Frenchs Forest, NSW p.683

Luke chapter 9 contains three stories that illustrate this.

3.1 Use what the team has

In Luke 9:10-17 (NIV), when the disciples complained that the crowd of 5,000 men plus women and children who had gathered to listen to him preaching were hungry, Jesus throws it back to the disciples. *"You give them something to eat,"* he says to them. They find five loaves of bread and two fish and Jesus takes what they have found and multiplies it. This feeds the group with twelve baskets full of scraps. Jesus takes what they offered and feeds the masses - the disciples were empowered because it was their offering that Jesus took and multiplied.

The first lesson in empowerment - **find out what your team has to offer and use it**, however small that may be. This includes their ideas on how to do things.

3.2 Give them authority

In Luke 9: 1-6 and 10, Jesus sends out the disciples with his authority to preach the kingdom of God, heal the sick and drive out demons. He gave them instructions to depend on the hospitality of the villagers they met along the way, or to leave that town if there was no hospitality offered. When they had done this they returned and reported back to Jesus what they had done. They had seen Jesus' authority in action and seen him at work in ministry doing these same things, and now it was their turn to put what they had learnt into practice. Luke 10:17 (NIV) records that they reported, *"Lord, even the demons submit to us in your name."*

They discovered the next lesson in empowerment - **give them your authority to act.** When people are given the authority of their leader or manager, they know they are now operating at a higher level of accountability than their own, and that is empowering for them. It must be done with accountability back to the manager though so that mistakes can be corrected.

3.3 Make failures learning experiences

Thirdly, in Luke 9:37-43 (NIV), a father brings his son to Jesus. The boy is possessed by an evil spirit but the father explains that, *"I begged your disciples to drive it out, but they could not."* Jesus chides the people as being an *"unbelieving and perverse generation"* but then goes ahead to rebuke the evil spirit and heal the boy. The crowd was immediately *"amazed at the greatness of God."* Perhaps a little frustrated at the disciples inability to drive out this evil spirit, Jesus nevertheless goes ahead to give another lesson in ministry and restores the boy. The needed to see Jesus demonstrate it again before they were confident to do it themselves.

Was this empowering for the disciples? What happens when we make mistakes or fail to deliver? Empowering our team members must continue even when they fail. Jesus laments that he still needs to be around them for a while longer. He knows they still have more to learn and so he goes ahead with another ministry lesson and drives out the demon.

So here is another principle in empowering people - **make failure a learning experience**, not a disciplinary experience.

QUESTIONS FOR DISCUSSION

1. In what ways was the method the author used to find out the worker's preferences empowering to them? What else could he have done? How would you have felt if you were one of those workers?

2. What style of leadership do you prefer to use when leading a team (be honest with yourself!)?

3. Review the three points for empowering people above (from Luke 9). How can you practically use these in your own management work - think of specific ways you can do that now with current projects?

4. What new thing have you learnt about empowering people? How can you implement this in your own leadership style?

5. How is empowering leadership different from your traditional management and cultural models of leadership?

4. Servant Leadership

It was just before the Passover Feast. Jesus knew that the time had come for him to leave this work and go to the Father. Having loved his own who were in the world, he now showed them the full extent of his love.

The evening meal was being served, and the devil had already prompted Judas Iscariot, son of Simon, to betray Jesus. Jesus knew that the Father had put all things under his power, and that he had come from God and was returning to God; so he got up from the meal, took off his outer clothing and wrapped a towel around his waist. After that he poured water into a basin and began to wash the disciples' feet, drying them with the towel that was wrapped around him.   John 13:1-5 (NIV).

※

Jesus' empowering leadership is an example of his servant leadership style. While using the words "power" and "servant" may seem contradictory, in fact the secret of Jesus' power lay in his servanthood. We'll touch on a few aspects of that servanthood here.

Philippians 2:1-11 is a critical passage in understanding the servanthood of Jesus. Humility is a key word. Jesus, despite being God in nature and therefore entitled to use his position as one with God, *"did not consider equality with God something to be grasped (or held onto) but made himself nothing, taking the very nature of a servant, being made in human likeness."* (Philippians 2: 6-7 NIV)

So while Jesus was all powerful in the sense that he was God's son, he put that aside to become nothing, a mere human being, a servant. What he did maintain was his obedience to God, an obedience that led to his death on the cross. In his ministry, Jesus used the authority given to him by God (the Father), an authority that was complete because of his total commitment and obedience to do what his Father desired (see John 14:9-14).

The early verses of Philippians 2 (NIV) speak of the attitude of servanthood that Jesus embodied.

vs 3 *"Do nothing out of selfish ambition or vain conceit but in humility consider others better than yourselves."*

vs 4 *"Each of you should look not only to your own interests, but also to the interests of others."*

vs 5,7 *"Your attitude should be the same as that of Christ Jesus ...who made himself nothing, taking the very nature of a servant."*

Jesus in his earthly ministry did not function in leadership from his position of authority as the king of the universe but humbled himself, placing others as the focus of his life and sacrificial death. In doing so, he fulfilled the Father's desire to provide the way for all people to enter into the kingdom of God through faith in him, now that the blockage of sin and disobedience had been dealt with at the cross. Release from sin and satan's grip on our mind and body is absolute empowerment, only possible because of Jesus' willingness to give up his nature as God and become human.

"Since the children have flesh and blood, he too shared in their humanity so that by his death he might destroy him who holds the power of death - that is the devil - and free those who all their lives were held in slavery by their fear of death." (Hebrews 2:14-15 NIV)

Washing the disciples feet

Jesus acted out this servanthood in different ways with his disciples. None is more startling than what is recorded in John chapter 13 (NIV), when Jesus washes his disciples feet. The context of this event is important and significant. John records this as Jesus showing his disciples *"the full extent of his love"* for them (vs 1). It is the start of the Passover Feast and Jesus is meeting with his disciples in a secretive place so that they would not be discovered easily.

Jesus already knew that Judas was about to betray him within an hour or two. *"Jesus knew that the Father had put all things under his power, and that he had come from God and was returning to God, so he got up from the meal, took off his outer garment, and wrapped a towel around his waist."* (vs 3-4). Jesus' action to wash the disciples' feet and demonstrate absolute servanthood seems to flow directly from his understanding now of his God given authority and approaching death. It was a very deliberate act.

In the culture of that time, when visitors entered a house, the host would arrange for their feet to be washed to remove the dust and dirt from walking outside on dusty roads. This was a task allocated for servants to do, it was not something a house host would do himself. Jesus very symbolically identifies himself in the servant role, washing each one's feet and drying them with the towel around his waist.

The meaning in this is profound given that John tells us (vs 2) that Judas the betrayer was present. Jesus was very aware that Judas was now committed to betray him, prompted by the devil. Jesus humbles himself as a servant even to Judas who would shortly betray him, something he eludes to as he teaches them further about what he has just done (vs 11).

"'Do you understand what I have just done for you,' he asked them. 'You call me Teacher and Lord and rightly so, for that is what I am. Now that I, your Lord and Teacher, have washed your feet, you also should wash one another's feet. I have set you an example that you should do as I have done for you.'" (vs 12-15)

While the literal exercise of washing each other's feet is humbling, what is Jesus really talking about here? Even though he was now well acknowledged as a Teacher (Rabbi) and Lord, he sets the benchmark for humility and servanthood by **washing even his enemies feet**. To do what Jesus does and follow his example has profound implications in how we treat not only our friends but also our enemies and those who turn against us.

How do we apply this to leadership at a management level? The extent to which Jesus treated all people the same is enviable. We are so easy affected by whether people are supportive of us or not, whether we feel they like us or not, and whether we perceive they are willing to listen to and follow us or not. Or even try to stab us in the back. The servant leader rises above these perceptions to serve all without compromise or distraction. All are included in the servant leader's willingness to empower and equip.

The Marks of a Servant Leader

In more practical terms:
- The servant leader has the ability to lead a group of people to achieve their goals and the ability to lead a group of people to achieve all that God wishes them to achieve.
- The servant leader seeks to draw people to follow by honouring and empowering them with respect, always

lifting people up to achieve their potential.
- The servant leader acts like a servant of God to serve others.
- The servant leader recognises that God has given him or her this responsibility to develop their team members' potential so they can together serve their organisation and God.
- The servant leader sees his or her team members as potentials, not problems.
- The servant leader treats all people equally, extending the same opportunity to each.

※

> TO LEAD THE PEOPLE, WALK BEHIND THEM. FOR THE BEST LEADERS, PEOPLE DO NOT NOTICE THEIR EXISTENCE. WHEN THE BEST LEADER'S WORK IS DONE, THE PEOPLE SAY "WE DID IT OURSELVES"
>
> Chinese philosopher Lao-Tsu (6th Century BC)

QUESTIONS FOR DISCUSSION

1. What do you think you would be feeling if you were one of the disciples as Jesus washed your feet? How would that change your attitudes about leadership and power?

2. What attitudes or rules are preventing managers from exercising servant leadership in your organisation?

3. When you consider the marks of a servant leader, would you consider that you are a servant leader? What marks do you need to improve on?

4. Do you have any issues with any of your team members that prevents you from 'washing their feet', serving them in humility and accepting them?

5. What are the marks of a servant leader in your culture or community?

5. Communication and Listening

Joe was the operations manager for a company which employed staff as shift workers. It was always a challenge to make sure he rostered enough workers for each shift and he put a lot of time into making sure the weekly roster was complete.

After two staff called in sick, Joe had to make a change to the roster, so he researched all the possibilities and decided to bring Sophie's shift next day forward from 1pm to 8am. After finalising the revised roster, he printed it off and pinned it on the staff notice board for all to see.

Next day he was surprised that Sophie had not come to work at 8am. She was always prompt and on time. In fact she did not come in until 1pm. Joe asked her into his office to discuss this.

"Sophie, how come you came to work late today?" he asked her, frustrated because he had to step in to help the rest of the team work harder that morning to make up for her absence.

"No boss," she replied, " I didn't come to work late, my roster was for 1pm start."

"No it wasn't, it was for 8am," said Joe. "Why didn't you come in at 8?"

"Boss, my roster says 1pm," said Sophie and pulled out her old roster schedule from her pocket to show him.

"But there is an updated roster that I put on the notice board yesterday. Don't you read the notice board before you go home?"

"Yes, I always read the notice board boss, and I didn't see that update. What time did you put it up there?" asked Sophie, not in a mood to argue with the boss.

"Just after 3pm I put it there," replied Joe, pointing to the notice board with his finger.

"Boss," said Sophie, "my shift finished at 3pm yesterday so I didn't see anything posted there after 3. How do you expect me to know about a shift change when you don't advise me when I am here at work?" Sophie's tone of voice changed. She was annoyed that Joe had not communicated the change to her properly.

⋊

Leadership is primarily about relationships, as we have noted already. The main way we manage those relationships is through communication. Without some form of communication, relationships wither and die. The type of communication we use has a profound affect on what kind of relationship we build. For example, domineering communication in all its forms builds relationships of power and subservience, reinforcing the authority of the manager, maintaining the employee in a state of subservience. But it may not build relationships of trust or respect. If our goal is to empower our employees in the best interests of the organisation and the individual, what communication tools are going to best achieve that?

First of all we need to consider what constitutes effective communication. While words form an important part of communication, there are many other factors which affect the correct transmission of meaning. The goal of communication is to transmit the MEANING of a message, so that the person receiving the message fully understands that meaning. That may be as simple as "turn left now", or as complex as a one hour lecture on "how an aircraft wing generates lift". The SENDER of the message encodes the message into a FORM which is then transmitted to the

RECEIVER, who decodes the form to receive the meaning of the message. Language is a primary message 'form' - if I speak to you in a language you do not understand, then I have used the wrong form and you will not understand the correct message.

But many other factors also influence the communication of a message, such as body language, intonation, context and feelings. If I am feeling discouraged, I am more likely to interpret your message negatively. If you are smiling when you discipline me, I may think you are joking or humouring me and understand the wrong message.

Similar forms can also convey different messages depending on the context. For example, what meaning is conveyed by flashing car headlights? In PNG if another car flashes headlights at you, it probably means it is a wantok (friend) who has recognised you, or another driver signalling for you to proceed in front of them. In Australia, flashing headlights on the highway can mean there is a Police radar trap ahead, or if at an intersection, it can be signalling another driver to come first while you wait. However in the Philippines, as I experienced it, flashing headlights at an intersection can mean that you are telling the other driver that you are coming through first! Getting the wrong message can have disastrous results!

A critical component of communication is the FEEDBACK loop. While a sender may transmit their message, they have no way of knowing whether the correct meaning was received by the receiver unless there is some form of communication back to the sender. Communication technically has not happened until the sender can confirm that the correct meaning of the message has been received and understood. Email is one of the worst offenders in this. How often does someone send an email and then think that they have communicated? Until you receive an email or phone call back from the receiver to advise that they have received the correct message, you cannot presume that communication has happened.

This diagram illustrates the communication and feedback loop:

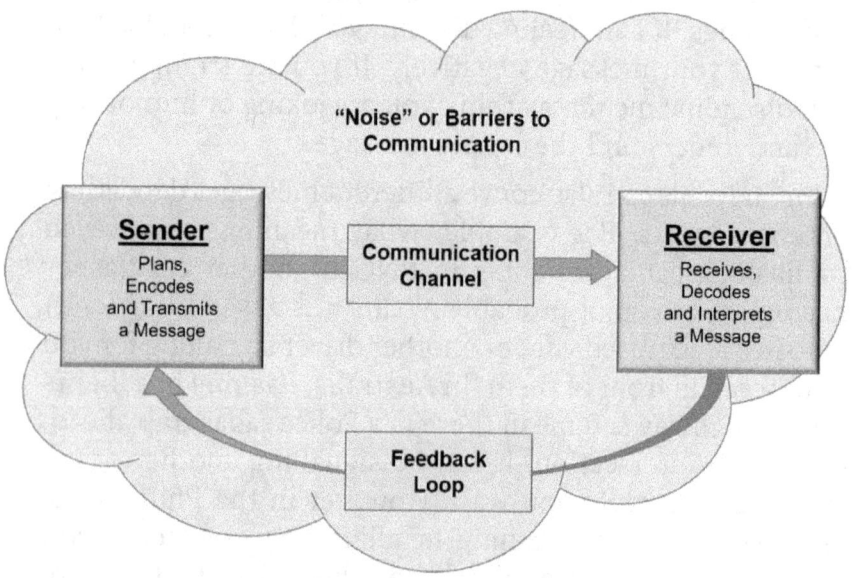

The most effective communication then recognises that the **form** of communication must be able to be recognised by the receiver. So the most effective form of communication must be based on what the receiver knows and will understand, not what the sender knows.

I am a pilot and flying instructor. I have taught high school students to fly, and conducted professional check and training with highly experienced pilots in PNG field operations. When communicating flight principles to 15 year old high school students, I will use a different style of language and presentation than I will when doing training for an experienced, mature age commercial pilot. If I speak to mature experienced pilots the same way as high school students having their first flight, the mature pilots will think I am treating them like children! How will this affect the actual meaning I want to communicate to them? To start with they may be put off by me treating them like a novice and so won't actually be listening to what I am saying, so that becomes a barrier to good communication.

God's Communication Strategy

How does this relate to the Bible? Well, let's ask the question, what was God's communication strategy when he wanted to communicate the most important message of salvation to mankind? We know that God could have asked angels to conduct a leaflet drop telling us about his plan to save us. Or he could have painted the message in clouds across the sky. There are any number of ways he could have communicated to us. But what did he choose to do?

There are a number of verses that tell the answer to this. We have already mentioned Philippians 2:7-8, *"... being made in human likeness, and being found in appearance as a man..."* John 1:14 says simply that *"the Word became flesh and made his dwelling among us."* Hebrews 2:14 states, *"Since the children have flesh and blood, he too shared in their humanity..."* (NIV)

Jesus Christ, the one who would become the means of salvation, became a human because that was the best way that mankind could understand the meaning of the message. The message of salvation came through the form of Jesus as a human being so that we could best understand it. God placed his message in the most appropriate form that we, the receivers, could understand - being human.

Hebrews 2:18 (NIV) adds, *"Because he himself [that is, Jesus] suffered when he was tempted, he is able to help those who are being tempted."* This is referred to as the incarnation. The basis of the incarnation is that God in Christ became a man so that he could reach mankind. When we see Jesus as a human being, we understand the message. For example:

- When we recognise that he lived a sinless life, we understand that he can be the one who frees us from our sinful life.
- When we see how he forgave those who killed him, we understand how God can forgive us for the wrong against him we have done.
- When we read of how Jesus lived as a man and hear his teachings, we discover a different way of living that we can embrace to honour God in our lives.
- When we know from the eye witness testimonies of the disciples that Jesus was resurrected and now sits with God in heaven, we know that we too will be resurrected to join Jesus in the kingdom of heaven.

What about the feedback loop? The Bible has many references to this as well. John 1:12 says that *"to all who received him, to those who believed in his name, he gave the right to become the children of God…"* Peter, preaching on the day of Pentecost in Acts 2:38 says, *"Repent and be baptised in the name of Jesus Christ for the forgiveness of your sins…"* (NIV)

How does God know we have received the meaning of the message clearly? The act of repentance, receiving Christ, believing in him, baptism… these are all acts in response to the message we have received. These are the feedback loop in action which tell God that we have received and understood, and are taking action which confirms that.

Listening

Have you ever wondered why we were created with two ears and one mouth? While our ears play a vital role in other functions of our body apart from hearing, such as balance, and our mouth for taste and eating as well as talking, I like to think that it reminds us of our need to listen more than talk.

Listening is one of the key skills to being a good communicator. For most people it is a skill that we have to learn. As a leader and manager, it is your ability to listen to your staff that will set you apart in their estimation of your leadership ability. Too often when we are speaking with some one else we are thinking only about what we are going to say, especially when there is a conflict. But the result is that we are not really listening to the other person. I have had to watch my own tendency to jump in on top of the other person when they are speaking, cutting them off because I want to say my words. You may also identify with that.

Here are several techniques to become a good listener:

- Whenever you start a conversation, in your mind establish that listening is your first priority, not trying to get your point of view across.
- Make sure your body language, your expression, how you are seated or standing, the amount of background noise, and so on, are a help to establishing a listening environment. Identify and eliminate distractions - the other person must know that you are giving them 100% attention. Watching State of Origin 3 on the TV when trying to have a serious conversation will not work!
- Whenever you are tempted to jump in on top of the other person and cut them off, check yourself and

deliberately hold back until they have finished their sentence or point.

- Listen empathetically - put yourself in their shoes so you can really understand what they are saying. This means you give up your rights to be correct or to have your solution as the only one. You are listening so that you really start to feel you understand their point of view and why, whether you agree or disagree with them. A Native American Indian expression goes like this: *"To truly understand another, we must walk a mile in their moccasins, and before we can walk in another's moccasins, we must first take off our own."*

- Make sure the other person feels that they are in control of the conversation when they are talking. Stephen Covey[2] illustrates this with the example of an 'Indian Talking Stick' he was given by American Indians. Any item can be substituted for the carved walking stick he has. The point is that whoever is holding the item is in control of the conversation and the other person will not interrupt except to clarify what they understand is being said. When the person with the 'talking stick' feels that they are understood, they hand it to the other person who now has control of the conversation and continues until they feel understood by the other. And so it goes on until both parties feel fully understood by the other person.

Once you both understand each other fully, you are in a position to come to a conclusion, fix the problem or brainstorm a solution as the case may be.

---

[2]. in Stephen Covey, *7 Habits of Highly Effective People,* Free Press USA 1989..

QUESTIONS FOR DISCUSSION

1. Why did Joe's attempt to communicate fail? Explain that in terms of the communication loop diagram. What could he have done better to make sure there was efficient communication with Sophie?

2. How can you apply the communication feedback loop to make sure you always get feedback as a manager? List the various forms of communication you use and how you can get or give feedback.

3. How often does poor communication and misunderstanding result in problems (tension between people, wrong instructions etc) in the workplace?

4. Think of a situation in your workplace where you have not practiced good listening skills. What can you do next time to demonstrate better listening skills?

5. How can you apply listening with empathy next time you meet with a staff member?

6. Resolving Conflict

Julie was a good Office Manager at her company. As it was a small company she was also the front office Receptionist. Part of her duties was to greet, assist and monitor everyone who came through the front door as well as answer the phone. She also managed use of the photocopier which was located in the main office, not the reception area. She loved her job but at times it was very busy especially when Board meetings were approaching and the General Manager required additional photocopying of Board reports.

This was the situation recently when both the GM and Finance Manager called her to request she urgently photocopy reports for an unplanned Board meeting which had been called for the next day. Julie advised that she was very happy to do it but in her mind she knew that it would be hard to monitor the front door and telephone if she was busy at the photocopier for a long period of time. So she explained this to the GM and FM, who acknowledged her, saying that would be fine.

She was however, able to complete all the copying and staple the reports about half an hour before knock off time, and so she was satisfied she had done a good job.

The day after the Board meeting, her direct boss, the Administration Manager, called her into the office and began to speak to her in a negative tone of voice.

"I need you to explain why you were not in the office to monitor the front door two days ago," the Admin Manager asked, directly confronting Julie, and sounding very upset. She continued, "I have had a very sharp email from one of our best customers who

Leading to Empower

is angry that they could not get into the office because the door was shut and no-one was there to let them in. They even said they tried to phone several times and even the phone was not being answered. You know that is your responsibility and so I want to know why you were not doing your duties. This is a very serious breach of your duties and may have cost us the business of one of our best customers. Do you understand how serious this is?" The Admin Manager's voice had been getting higher and higher and louder and louder as she spoke.

Julie was by now quite intimidated and struggled to know how to respond.

"I was here ... but .... busy with other things," she managed to say, trying to maintain her composure, though she thought the manager would have seen her hands shaking.

"Well that's not good enough and not an excuse, you failed in your duties and I will have to take disciplinary action," declared the Admin Manager. *"Don't let me ever catch you not being here in the reception area and able to monitor the door and answer the phone again, or you'll need to look for another job... if you still have one that is!"* With that, she turned and walked away from Julie.

⋇

Listening empathetically is critically important when trying to resolve conflict. Conflict is defined in the Cambridge English Dictionary as *"an active disagreement between people with opposing opinions or principles"*[3]. It is very difficult to work with someone in your team, church or club who has opposing ideas, opinions and even principles than you have. If you are their manager, how can you resolve the conflict so that you can work together in harmony?

---
3. https://dictionary.cambridge.org › dictionary › english › conflict

It is worth noting that workplace research indicates that reduced conflict in a team or work environment results in greater productivity. If people are experiencing less stress and are happier, they will do their job better. This is true for any environment where people are together whether it is work, family, church or club. So reducing conflict in your team will result in better performance of your team.

In an article titled Proof That Positive Work Cultures Are More Productive,[4] the authors give this advice to leaders:

- **Foster social connections** – research shows positive social connections at work produce highly desirable results. For example, people get sick less often, recover twice as fast from surgery, experience less depression, learn faster and remember longer, tolerate pain and discomfort better, display more mental acuity, and perform better on the job. Toxic, stress-filled workplaces affect social relationships and, consequently, life expectancy.

- **Show Empathy** - leaders who demonstrate compassion toward employees foster individual and collective resilience in challenging times.

- **Go out of your way to help** - when leaders are not just fair but self-sacrificing, their employees are actually moved and inspired to become more loyal and committed themselves. As a consequence, they are more likely to go out of their way to be helpful and friendly to other employees, thus creating a self-reinforcing cycle.

- **Encourage people to talk to you** – especially about their problems. Not surprisingly, trusting that the leader has your best interests at heart improves employee performance.

---

[4]. Emma Sapala and Kim Drake, Proof That Positive Work Cultures Are More Productive, *Harvard Business Review*, Dec 10, 2015

These all relate to how the leader communicates in various forms to reduce conflict, noting that conflict has many serious negative effects within the life of the team and the personal lives of the team members.

Paul and Barnabas

The story of Paul and Barnabas recorded in the Book of Acts gives us an example of the reality of conflict. Both were selected by the church in Antioch to spearhead the outreach of the church further afield (Acts 13). So they set out on what is known as Paul's first missionary journey, with verse 5 noting that John accompanied them as a helper. In Acts 13:13 the writer, Luke, adds a note that at Perga in Pamphylia John (also known as Mark) left them to return to Jerusalem. At this stage we have no real idea of why John Mark left the group or under what circumstances. After some time Paul and Barnabas returned to Antioch to report back to their sending church.

Acts 16:36 (NIV) records that *"some time later Paul said to Barnabas, 'Let us go back and visit the brothers in all the towns where we preached the word of the Lord and see how they are doing.'"* But a disagreement arose between them because Barnabas wanted to take John Mark, while Paul didn't think it wise to do so, *"because he had deserted them in Pamphylia"*. Acts 16:38 (NIV). Neither man gave in to the other and so Barnabas took John Mark with him and left for Cyprus, while Paul chose Silas to accompany him back to the churches in Syria and Cilicia.

Barnabas, real name Joseph, was named Barnabas, 'son of encouragement', by the disciples in Acts 4:36 when he sold a field and donated the money to the early church leaders. By his role in the early church though it is clear he was the

Leading to Empower

kind of person who took opportunities to personally bring encouragement to others. John Mark was his cousin[5] and so we can understand Barnabas' desire to support his cousin. We know Paul in his former days as Saul was a Jewish religious zealot and probably a hard man. So both held onto their convictions and as a result, they split up as a team and went different directions. Paul seemed to have little time for John Mark whereas Barnabas (the encourager) believed John Mark still had potential and so he took him under his wing again. We don't know the reason for the disagreement over John Mark but it possibly relates to John Mark feeling uncomfortable about the mission that was more and more reaching out to Gentiles rather than Jews.

Many years later, when writing to Timothy from prison, Paul encourages Timothy to come and visit him because many of his friends had now deserted him. In 1 Timothy 4:11, Paul asks Timothy to *"get Mark and bring him with you because he is helpful in my ministry."* (NIV) We have little extra information recorded about John Mark in the interim but from this comment alone we can appreciate that Paul had changed his mind about John Mark and now welcomed him and his ministry.

There must have been a reconciliation between them. I can only presume that when they met again, John Mark was able to explain why he left the team at Pamphylia and an understanding of the situation allowed Paul to forgive him and now consider him of great value in the ministry. In that sense, Barnabas' willingness to keep encouraging John Mark may have been essential in that process, saving him from dropping out altogether. In fact, John Mark went on to write the gospel of Mark, making his contribution to the historical record of the life and ministry of Jesus. Reconciliation leads to benefits for both sides.

---

5. Colossians 4:10

Principles for conflict resolution

Unfortunately we don't have any biblical record of how the reconciliation between Paul and John Mark took place, or between Paul and Barnabas. But there are principles that you can use as a manager and leader to facilitate a resolution in time of conflict. These principles apply whether in a personal, work, church, club or home environment. Of course it takes willingness by both parties first of all to agree to discuss the issue, but beyond that, there needs to be agreement to listen to each other without bias. The following steps may be of help to leaders and managers as a process to resolve conflict:

1. **Arrange to meet and discuss the situation with the other person.** As a manager you can easily arrange this if the person is a staff member on your team. Make sure you allocate their duties to someone else if needed so they can be free. It is important that you give a brief idea of what you want to discuss, for example, "I want to discuss the situation about the decision I made which you disagreed with." You must be careful to use non-judgemental language.

2. At the meeting **explain the situation briefly as you perceive it and why it is important to resolve it.** Again, using non-judgemental language is critical. As soon as you use words that are accusing the other person, then you have lost them and the ability to discuss the situation openly. Do not use "you" phrases or sentences, for example, "You have not finished your work and you left early yesterday" is accusing the person, to which they will react negatively to defend themself. To rephrase that to say, "Your time sheet indicates that you went home half an hour early yesterday and I was concerned that some work elements were not

completed on time," expresses the facts and your own feelings about the result as it affected you as manager. The person can now respond to this factually without feeling that you are accusing them of something.

3. Now open the discussion up and **invite them to respond and tell you their story. Listen empathetically** and carefully, give them the talking stick, or rock or whatever you have, and ask questions but only to clarify your understanding of their point of view. Do not interrupt or argue with them but allow them to speak until they are ready to allow you to share your point of view. Make sure that in your communication, both of you fully understand the other person's point of view before moving on.

4. Now **summarise the problem to discover what the real issue is.** Sometimes that means asking WHY several times to get to the bottom of it. This is a technique used by accident investigators to get to the root cause of an accident but it applies in any situation where you are seeking to dig deeper into the issue. Asking follow up questions such as, "Why did you decide to take that action?" or "Why did this make you feel that way?" can help you understand the other person's situation better.

5. In any conflict **you want a WIN-WIN solution, so try and find it.** In other words, both sides feel they have achieved what they are seeking. It may mean some compromise on both sides, and it will often mean finding a common solution which is different and new compared to the ideas each party held. But once you both understand each other, you can approach the situation together seeking a common solution.

6. You may have to think through several possible solutions before agreeing on one. Evaluate each one

together so that **the final solution you agree on** is good and will work well for both of you.

7. Once you agree on a solution, then you will need to decide how best to implement it. **So agree on an action plan** with time frames. If you are a manager dealing with a staff member, then arrange for another follow up meeting to make sure you are both implementing it satisfactorily.

QUESTIONS FOR DISCUSSION

1. How would you describe the meeting between Julie and her manager? Retell or rewrite this story with the Admin Manager demonstrating good empathetic listening skills? What would be different about the outcome if the Manager had listened to Julie?

2. Describe a conflict situation you have experienced as a manager. Did you achieve a win-win solution or did it end unsatisfactorily?

3. How hard is it to apply empathetic listening skills in a conflict situation which has become an argument?

4. Apply the 5 principles above to the situation Julie faced and see if the situation can be resolved satisfactorily. Once there is a good understanding of both sides, then potential solutions can be explored. What would some of those solutions be in this situation?

5. Think of a situation where a conflict may arise in your workplace or team. How can you apply the 5 principles for conflict resolution above to that situation?

7. Managing Job Performance

*J*eff, the business owner, prided himself on having clean facilities in his business. Floors always swept, rubbish bins emptied regularly and bathroom and toilets always being clean with good stocks of toilet paper and hand towels. At least once a day he would actually do a personal inspection of the bathrooms to make sure everything was in good order. His business had a lot of clients coming into the office. He wanted the cleanliness of the facilities to demonstrate the commitment to excellence that he wanted his clients to feel about the business.

He had recently taken on a new cleaner, Andros, who came with very good references. He had shown Andros around the building and pointed out where everything was, and then let him start working. But on an inspection this morning he had found the toilet paper and hand towels had run out. He decided to monitor the situation more closely and found that they were still empty at a 3pm inspection.

He called Andros into his office to talk with him about it.

"I have inspected the bathrooms twice today Andros, and you didn't clean the washroom or put in new paper towels or toilet paper. You came with very good references but I feel like you are not really very good as a cleaner if you can't see that you need to replace papers when they run out," said Jeff.

Andros was surprised that within a week of starting work he was already in trouble with the boss! He didn't know what to say so stayed silent, looking at the floor.

Jeff saw that Andros was embarrassed and realised he had not started the conversation well.

"I'm sorry, I didn't mean to start like that," he said. "I really appreciated having you join our company. You will know already that I only like the best and so when I read your references, I knew I was getting the best cleaner in town. Thank you for coming to work with us. However there is a matter we need to talk about. When I inspected the bathroom I saw that the hand towels and toilet papers were empty. This is a performance gap. Can you tell me what's happened that you were not able to refill them? I'm sure you would have done your best to fix it. Tell me what your story is please."

Andros realised that the boss genuinely wanted to know what had happened and was not now blaming him, so he explained,

"Boss, I am so sorry that you found the bathrooms in that condition. When I took over the cleaner job here last week there were hardly any stocks of hand towels and toilet papers in the cupboard. As you know, I didn't get a handover-takeover briefing from the previous cleaner, and I never received any information about how to get new supplies of papers. To be honest, it worried me for the first two days here and I hardly slept at night worrying about it!" Andros took a deep breath before continuing.

"So by the time I found out from another worker here that there was a process to order new stock from the company Stores, it was too late because they take 5 days to get the stocks in. They don't actually keep enough stocks in supply. So I couldn't do anything until the new stocks arrived just before you called me in." Andros was glad to get this off his chest now.

"Well, that certainly explains the situation Andros, thank you for being honest, I can fully understand now, and I want to apologise to you for placing you in this situation. Tell me, how do you think we can avoid this happening again in future?" asked Jeff.

Andros was pleased that his boss was actually asking him for advise, it made him feel good.

"Well Boss, to start with I need to have an information sheet that gives me a process and time frame for ordering new supplies. I don't even know how much I can spend so a budget for cleaning supplies will really help me make sure I use materials efficiently."

Jeff was starting to realise that Andros actually was a pretty smart worker and wanted to manage his work well.

"I actually don't even have a job description," continued Andros, "so when you said there was a performance gap, I wasn't sure what you meant because I don't have a job description or any KPIs to measure performance. I'm sorry to point this out and do so respectfully." Andros wondered if he had overstepped his boundary with the boss.

"Andros, I really appreciate your honesty, in fact I want you to feel free to knock on my door anytime you have any ideas. I can see that I have failed you by not giving you a comprehensive induction including a job description with KPI's. Would you be able to work with me tomorrow for a few hours while we work out your job description together, because you know cleaning work better than I do, and I like your ideas?" asked Jeff.

Andros couldn't believe what his boss was saying.

"Is there anything else you want to say Andros?" asked Jeff, keen to make sure he gave Andros every opportunity to express himself.

"There is, Boss, if you don't mind. The kind of chemicals you are using, they are rubbish and not good for the environment. Can I suggest a much better chemical that is also better environmentally and may even be cheaper for you?" offered Andros, realising that his relationship with Jeff was now empowering both of them and helping the company.

"That's a great suggestion Andros, let's look at that in more detail tomorrow then." He paused. "By the way, you are already a great asset to the company, I'm so glad I hired you."

Andros just smiled as he left the office.

In Chapter 1 we noted that God the Manager gave clear directions to newly created man, as well as set boundaries for him and his partner within the garden of Eden. In some ways we can liken these instructions to a basic job description and performance goals for Adam.

"Be fruitful and increase in number, fill the earth and subdue it. Rule over the fish of the sea and the birds of the air and over every living thing that moves on the ground." Genesis 1:28 (NIV). A little later God instructed Adam that, *"you are free to eat from any tree in the garden but you must not eat from the tree of the knowledge of good and evil..."* Genesis 2:16-17 (NIV).

Within their 'job description' to increase in number and rule over the rest of the created animal kingdom, they were able to eat of any tree in the garden except the tree of the *"knowledge of good and evil"*. Their performance measure was to refrain from eating from this specific tree. Unfortunately they didn't achieve the performance target God set them, and suffered the consequences - exclusion from the garden, and the curse of disobedience upon all mankind since then! While people have debated what kind of tree it was, I think it must have been a mango! There is nothing as luscious as a freshly ripened mango on the tree! But that's just my opinion!

In another Bible passage, Matthew 10, Jesus sends out his twelve disciples to conduct ministry. He gives them authority, his own authority, to conduct the ministry of preaching, healing the sick and driving out demons. Their job description is quite detailed, as we read from Matthew 10:5ff (NIV):

"Do not go among the Gentiles or enter any town of the Samaritans. Go rather to the lost sheep of Israel. As you go, preach this message: 'the kingdom of heaven is near'. Heal the sick, raise the dead, cleanse those who have leprosy, drive out demons. Freely you have received,

freely give. Do not take along any gold or silver or copper in your belts; take no bag for the journey, or extra tunic, or sandals or staff." Jesus continues to give them advice about accommodation options with villagers and how they should conduct themselves. The disciples left for their ministry experience with very clear expectations of what they were to do.

※

A manager's role is to organise the resources at hand, including the team, and provide direction to ensure that the organisation's goals are met, at least in the section or department for which that manager is responsible. As a leader, the focus is on empowering the team members to do their part, and part of that is ensuring the team members have the capability, capacity and authority they need. These roles of manager and leader are critical to working with your team to achieve the results required.

But clear communication about what they are required to do is essential. Without a clear job description, your team members will have little or no idea about what they should be doing. Unfortunately many organisations struggle to achieve their organisational goals and targets because their people do not have clear job descriptions.

Kris Cole[6] suggests that for people to perform their best, five key things must be in place:

1. People must know WHAT to do - job description
2. They must WANT to do it - motivation
3. They must know HOW to do it - training and skills
4. They must have a CHANCE to do it - job opportunity

---
6. Kris Cole, *Supervision - the Theory and Practice of First-Line Management* 2001, Prentice Hall, Frenchs Forest,NSW p.240

5. They must have effective LEADERSHIP and guidance - good supervision.

A good job description will clearly articulate the responsibilities of the worker, whatever level they are at, while also indicating any boundaries necessary. Respecting other co-worker's job descriptions is important. As a manager, make sure all your team have clear job descriptions.

Motivation is a key component of management and leadership. Keeping your team motivated will ensure they stay on track and you maintain their respect. Positive encouragement and feedback is so important as a motivator. When a manager recognises the value of a person's work, they are also recognising and affirming the value of that person. This builds self-confidence and esteem because the worker now knows they are able to do a good job at what they are doing. On the other hand, the absence of positive feedback usually means the worker only receives negative feedback, and this can be very destructive to their self-esteem, even to the point of them leaving the job. A manager who gives only negative feedback by complaining or making comments to put them down, or even just not saying anything positive, can destroy staff morale to the point where the best employees flee, and the remainder are demoralised.

As someone has said, *'people don't leave organisations, they leave managers'*.

Measuring Performance

If a worker does not have a clear job description, it is very difficult for them to know what they should be doing. So a fuzzy job description will result in workers doing what *they think* is what they should be doing, usually what they are most interested in, but it may not be what is required of them to achieve the organisation's goals. But with a clear job description and motivation, the question now is, how will the person know if they are doing a *good* job or not?

The need to receive appreciation and recognition for a job well done is one of the most important elements of good job performance.

> **THE DEEPEST PRINCIPLE OF HUMAN NATURE IS THE NEED TO BE APPRECIATED.**
> William James, psychologist

Key to measuring performance is to establish the criteria, targets, indicators or goals by which performance can be assessed. It is important that this process is not regarded as disciplinary in nature because disciplinary action, or even the hint of it, creates a defensive climate for the relationship between manager and staff member. It sends a message that the worker has done something wrong and that punishment is necessary. However when measuring performance, it is essential that the manager approaches it from the view point of seeking to help the worker achieve their target. Thus a performance management meeting between a manager and staff member will focus on identifying what performance gap exists between what the desired target is and what the actual performance of the person was, and how this gap can be reduced or eliminated.

Performance targets need to flow from each job description item and reflect a measurable goal. For example, if a cleaner has a job description item stating:

Leading to Empower

"Ensure toilet and wash room is clean and tidy",
the measurable performance indicator may be:

"Toilet and wash room floor mopped, toilet and sink cleaned with antiseptic wash, toilet and hand towel papers refilled, and rubbish bins emptied each day."

This target can be easily measured and supporting documentation could include a daily sign off sheet by the cleaner once completed.

Performance targets should be SMARTT:

- Specific and concise
- Measurable
- Achievable
- Related to overall organisational goals
- Time framed
- Tracked or easily monitored

Performance Gaps

If you as manager discover the wash room is not clean and paper towels not refilled one day, then you have established a performance gap - *the difference between the performance target* and *the worker's actual performance*. Here are examples:

```
PERFORMANCE STANDARD
Wear hi-vis vest at all times at work;
90% on time departures;
No unused drums at expiry date;
100% come to work on time;
Budget for cleaning fluid $200 per month;
All vehicles must have certified up to date First Aid kit
```

Perform.

Leading to Empower

Each of your team members, and you yourself, should be very clear about your job description and the associated performance indicators for each item.

When counselling someone to correct a performance gap, it is important that it is done in a non-judgemental way. One of the most negative ways to conduct such a session is to use "you" expressions. These are accusatory and come across as blaming the person for the lack of performance. In the above example of the cleaner, to say "you didn't clean the wash room or put in new paper towels," accuses the person and immediately puts them on the defensive. Rather, to say "when I visited the wash room and noted that the floor was dirty and there were no paper towels," advises them of the problem and de-personalises the issue, thus avoiding creating a conflict as result.

In a similar format to that proposed for dealing with conflict in the previous chapter, when meeting with the worker you are now in a position to discuss the problem as a performance gap between what is expected (performance target) and what happened (actual performance). It is no longer a personal issue. From recognition of the gap together, you can now proceed to discover the reason for the gap and then brainstorm solutions to help the person improve and reduce the gap.

ACTUAL PERFORMANCE

Hi-vis vest observed not worn twice;

82% on time departures;

12 drums still had fuel at expiry date;

Came late to work on 3 times;

Spent $245 on cleaning fluids last month;

Vehicle driven for 2 days without First Aid kit

The reasons for performance gaps are often complex. However poor performance is usually blamed on personal motivational factors. People are characterised as lazy, unmotivated, couldn't care, or some other negative personal attribute. But in reality, most poor performance is attributable to factors which are organisationally related. These can include:
- a poor job description,
- inadequate training,
- difficult or unnecessary procedures,
- a lack of information,
- poorly written documentation or instructions,
- the language of communication is not a first language,
- disharmony in the team,
- a lack of proper tools or other resources, and
- perhaps even that the person is just not suited to the job.

Factors which can contribute at a personal level can include the person's relationships at home or whether they have been sick.

Performance Management

Many organisations leave a performance review until an annual job appraisal is due. However, an appraisal does not fulfil the same function as a performance management review. In my experience, workers need to have regular reviews of their performance targets so that patterns can be established, and non-performance issues addressed in good time. For example, if a worker has had a performance gap in a particular task, you want to nip it in the bud quickly and guide the worker back to acceptable performance. So to meet monthly with your workers for a performance review is a good time frame. Otherwise, after 12 months, the gap has become a habit and it is much more difficult for the worker to change that behaviour.

I have found that a simple one page (landscape) template with columns as described below is a useful document to record gaps and agreed steps with the worker to improve. In the template, write in the job description items, then the associated SMARTT performance targets. These are best worked out with manager and worker together - the worker knows what is a reasonable target for them to achieve, the manager knows what standard they want the worker to achieve. It also gives the worker a sense of ownership of the targets, rather than something management is thrusting on them. Remember, we are always looking for ways to empower our staff. The more they feel in control, the more they feel empowered, and the better they will perform. At each subsequent monthly meeting, progress can be reviewed. It also provides a monthly record in the workers' file especially when no improvement occurs and disciplinary action needs to be considered.

I have a traffic light approach - OK is green, Improve is amber, and Not Ok is red. A tick in the appropriate column is all that is needed once the performance gap is identified and agreed upon. The final comments column allows for reporting on discussion and actions to improve.

Job Desc.	Perf. Targets	OK	Improve	NotOK	Comments

I also have a sign off section summarising agreed actions at the end of the document - both manager and worker need to sign and date, with a copy to the worker and to the manager/file.

In any performance management or counselling session the manager must take the time to fully investigate the root causes of the performance gap. Any causes that are an organisational responsibility, such as training or provision of adequate resources, should be addressed by the manager.

In the example of Andros the cleaner, if the company Stores have run out of paper towels and cannot provide them, then the gap can be seen as a larger organisational issue rather than just the cleaner's personal problem. However if the cleaner was off sick and didn't advise the manager who could then roster a replacement, then the performance gap related to not cleaning the wash room falls back to the responsibility of the cleaner for failing to communicate adequately with their manager. From establishing the facts of the reason for the gap, both the manager and worker now have matters to attend to, to reduce the gap in future - the manager will ensure Stores maintain a constant supply of paper towels, and the worker will remember to communicate when off sick.

At no stage is there any discussion about disciplinary measures. The focus is on helping the worker to achieve their performance targets. If however the worker is off sick again in future and fails to communicate this to the manager and the gap is repeated, then the manager will begin to consider how to deal with this under a disciplinary framework. This would probably mean advising the worker during the second performance management session that if they failed to communicate next time they were off sick, then they may need to be issued a first warning. But even the issue of a threat like this is designed to bring the worker back to improved performance, not to start punishing them! Serious disciplinary action is only valid once all attempts to correct the worker's poor performance have failed, and should always be in accordance with company policies.

One of the very motivating things that a manager can do is to recognise where the organisation has failed the worker, and then take positive steps to correct that. So, for example, if a worker advises that they are untrained for tasks required in their job description, it is empowering for the worker when the manager responds by acknowledging this and promptly schedules training for them. The same applies with tools and equipment. As a manager, always look for ways in which you can support your staff by up-skilling or resourcing them better.

Some time ago I was seeking to provide an upgraded level of training to some of my team. My proposal was considered too costly and rejected by senior management. While disappointing, it was the comment that I received at the time which concerned me more.

"If we train them more, they will only leave," I was told. I replied, "If we train them more, they will want to stay." Your attitude as a manager will make the difference.

QUESTIONS FOR DISCUSSION

1. How did Jeff change the whole tone of the discussion with Andros and turn it around? What was the impact of this for Andros - did it make much difference for him? How did Jeff successfully apply the 5 principles of communication in conflict situations?

2. How many times in the discussion did Jeff say something to provide positive feedback to Andros, appreciating Andros' value? How successful was it in motivating him?

3. Why do you think Andros did not feel he could tell Jeff about this situation earlier and so avoid a confrontation with Jeff his boss?

4. Is it a good idea to work together with your workers to build or review their job description? Why?

5. How can you manage performance gaps in your workplace without them becoming disciplinary in the first instance?

6. Can you note any performance gaps you now need to address with workers in your role as their manager, and think about how you will address them with the worker.

8. Delegation

Jimmy was a great mechanic. In his 20 years of experience with this transport company he had gained an incredible knowledge about every part of the workshop, and knew it. So he was excited when he was given the opportunity to become Workshop Manager. He knew his literacy and maths skills were not so good as he did not complete high school, but so far his limited skills in those areas had been enough for him as a mechanic.

Jimmy was a handyman as well and for a long time had been the self-proclaimed fix it man in the workshop, always tinkering and repairing things that needed it. In fact the other mechanics didn't even try and help out in that area because he didn't like it. They knew that he had a flash point and could easily get angry, so they knew the limits and when they should pull back and not get him angry.

Jimmy had a great sense of humour though and was really 'one of the boys' in the workshop, always ready to have a laugh and shoulder punch with the other mechanics. There were three other mechanics, all younger than Jimmy, so they respected him as an older workmate, as well as his temper. Being younger too, all of them had some understanding of computers and two of them had done Year 12 before learning their trade skills. One of them was always on his computer, though Jimmy never knew quite what he was doing. 'Learning code and software programming' he told Jimmy, which made no real sense to him anyway.

Now, four months into his new role as Workshop Manager,

Jimmy was floundering. It was not what he expected and the level of literacy and numeracy skills needed was much higher than he had or could hope to achieve. Trying to do a roster on a spreadsheet was impossible, let alone other computer based things the company was introducing, like invoices online. He had tried to keep up with what he was doing before so as not to appear lazy in the eyes of his colleagues. As well as that, the other three mechanics who he had got along with so well before had now turned on him, talking behind his back and refusing to cooperate with him sometimes, and not lifting a hand to help. He was doing his best but the Finance Manager was complaining that he was not keeping up with invoices and bills, and the General Manager was telling him that customers were complaining that the service level had dropped since he started as Workshop Manager. He was at a decision point - should he stay in the role or resign and ask to go back to being a mechanic again, or just resign altogether and retire? Was there another option? What could he do?

In Exodus 18 there is a great story which highlights another key tool for managers and leaders. The Hebrews who had escaped from Egypt were now encamped in the desert of Sinai. Little more than a year after they came out of Egypt, Moses conducted a census of the men over 20 who were eligible to join the army and fit to fight (see Numbers chapter 1). The count was 603,550 men (Numbers 2:46). So if we take into account that for every soldier there were probably at least 3 or 4 other family members, it is easy to estimate the total number of Hebrews at 3 or 4 million people or more.

Moses' father-in-law, Jethro, visits him and observes him sorting out disputes between the people, the sole judge for the group. He sees that Moses is going to burn out as he sits from dawn to dusk dealing with every complaint and conflict that arose. He wisely advises Moses:

"*What you are doing is not good. You and these people who come to you will wear yourselves out. The work is too heavy for you, you cannot handle it alone.*" Exodus 18:17-18 (NIV). Then he goes on to instruct Moses to pick "*capable men from all the people - men who fear God, trustworthy men who hate dishonest gain - and appoint them as officials over thousands, hundreds, fifties and tens. Have them serve as judges for the people at all times, but have them bring every difficult case to you; the simple cases they can decide themselves.*" Exodus 18:21-22 (NIV).

That way Moses could now use his time and energies better for his unique ministry to "*teach them the decrees and laws, and show them the way to live and the duties they are to perform.*" Exodus 18:20 (NIV).

Moses was wearing himself out and the timely advice of his father in law saved him from burnout and provided a better framework for him to manage his leadership duties.

It is common for managers to try and take on too much responsibility. It's easy to believe that you are the only one who can do the job properly. But recognising that as a manager you now have a team of people to work with and delegating the right duties can have some amazing benefits.

1. First of all it releases a load from the manager's shoulders and therefore helps reduce stress and, in doing so, reduce burnout.
2. It frees up the manager to be able to concentrate on duties which he or she can only do themselves, items that are part of their job description. Often these duties get put to one side and neglected while lesser duties are done.
3. It allows team members to take on more responsibility

and learn new skills. It is empowering to the team members because they are being trusted with more responsibility. The leaders who Moses chose were now being given leadership skills and experience they would not have learnt if Moses had not listened to his father in law.

Delegation is not something that can be taken lightly. First of all you have to make sure you have selected the right task to delegate. It is helpful to ask these questions first:

1. **Is this a task that I have to do or not?**
- Can someone else do it?

2. **Then you have to consider selecting the right person to do it:**
- Do any of my team already have the skills or experience to do this task?
- Are there people who I can train to do it?
- Do they have the time to do it or do I need to also reorganise their workload?
- Do I have the time and resources to train someone to do it?
- Can I afford for the task to be done poorly and do I have time to have it re-done if not satisfactory?

3. **Thirdly you have to ensure you delegate in the right way:**
- Do I have sufficient instructions for someone to understand what to do?
- Is the time frame available adequate for training, doing the task and then reviewing it?
- Do I have the time and availability to adequately supervise them?[7]

---
7. Original material in this chapter by Kevin White, used by permission.

Matina Jewell[8] is a senior manager who spent a number of years in the Australian Defence Force with primary roles in logistics. That included operating from naval ships "to move 1000 troops with six helicopters and 10 watercraft at night, with no lights and no radios to communicate." She says that the three key skills she had to learn were -

- "communicating effectively with my people,
- empowering them to make decisions at the right times,
- making sure I had the right people with the right skills to carry out the job."

Here is her reply when asked, "What are the key things leaders get wrong with delegation?"

She said, "They don't prepare themselves or their people correctly. You need to set clear objectives, define the parameters in which the team can operate and share a picture of what success actually looks like. You then need to define the resources to help get the job done. And crucially you need to establish formal and informal feedback groups, which allows the leader and the team to quickly evaluate, course-correct and keep the team on target to achieve the mission."

Good advice when considering delegation:

- prepare people,
- define objectives, parameters and success,
- define resources, and
- provide supervision through feedback mechanisms.

---

8. from Matina Jewell interview with Kirsten Galliot in *View from the Top*, QANTAS inflight magazine, p.114, early 2019.

Leading to Empower

QUESTIONS FOR DISCUSSION

1. Read over Jimmy's story again. What single thing could he do to save himself in his situation?

2. Why do you think Jimmy did not consider this himself?

3. Review the 3 sets of questions above and apply them to his situation. Do you think he could successfully proceed with this?

4. In your management role, can you think of some specific situations where you can delegate to someone in your team? What is stopping you from doing that?

5. What are the results of delegating for the manager, and for the worker?

9. Mentoring

Maria began to see a pattern in what was happening after about two months. Every two weeks, usually on a Friday morning, her old friend Konio would call her to have a chat. She always seemed to know what things might be challenging Maria in her work environment. Her advice and counsel was always gentle and shared from her own experience, and shared in a way which helped Maria to find solutions. In fact she had learnt to look forward to these discussions with Konio's obvious professional support for her as a colleague without actually intruding on her life in other areas. There again, she remembered that Konio had also worked for this same company here before being promoted and moving to a different town as a senior manager.

Now facing a real problem at work, Maria was finding it difficult to know how to proceed. Then she remembered Konio, and decided this time she would ring Konio for advice.

※

The stories of both Jesus and Paul in the New Testament are full of examples of their mentoring work. By mentoring I mean getting alongside someone in a relationship based role which provides guidance, learning and encouragement to develop the skills and experience sought in the designated discipline. Mentoring is usually an agreed role between two people, often for a specific period of time, such as a few months or a year or two or longer.

In chapter 7 we discussed the story of Jesus' sending the disciples out in ministry recorded in Matthew chapter 10. This was a vital phase of his mentoring of the disciples. The precursor to this though was up to three years of being together and sharing life, ministry experiences and teaching. Gradually Jesus taught them about the kingdom of God and demonstrated it through miracles and healings. Gradually he brought the disciples to the point where, to be able to really form the ministry potential in them, he sent them out alone, but with his authority. Remember, Jesus had just 3 years to develop a ministry team that would change the world! Then they reported back to him, establishing the feedback process so necessary in communication.

The relationship was personal. While at times they debated as to who Jesus really was, a rabbi, a prophet or the Messiah, it was not his teaching that kept them together, it was the relationship. Thrusting them out to solo ministry was a test of the trust that they had developed in Jesus, a trust based on what they learnt and experienced themselves under his tutelage. When Jesus decides that they have learnt all they need to know and sends them out with his authority, they know that they are empowered to do the same ministry as they have participated in while with him. When Jesus prepares to leave them but promises to send the Holy Spirit as a replacement, in his place (John 14:15-18), and then when they experience the empowerment of the Holy Spirit at Pentecost (Acts 2), as promised in Acts 1:8, they now continue their ministry in that same authority, fully empowered to do so, but now by themselves. The mentoring process with Jesus has taken them, in three years, from being in some cases, uneducated Jews, to being the bearers of the message of salvation to the world.

Paul's ministry in the book of Acts from chapter 13 onwards covers his adventures during three specific missionary journeys, and the events following on from them. The letters that he wrote to both the new churches he established and some of the people he mentored, give us many insights into his mentoring role.

From the start of his journeys, Paul takes on younger men as apprentices. We have already noted that John Mark accompanied Paul and Barnabas on the first trip, until he decided to leave them. Paul takes Silas with him on his second journey (Acts 15:40), and then at Lystra he meets a young man called Timothy, in whom Paul obviously recognises great potential. So he asks Timothy to join the team (Acts 16:1-3). We get a few glimpses of Paul's mentoring of Timothy during the second missionary journey. Initially Timothy is part of the team and we only read of Paul and Silas. But after visiting a number of provinces and cities, the team goes to Berea. Jews from Thessalonica follow them to Berea and begin to stir up trouble against Paul. So, *"the brothers immediately sent Paul to the coast, but Silas and Timothy stayed at Berea. The men who escorted Paul brought him to Athens and then left with instructions for Silas and Timothy to join him as soon as possible."* Acts 17:15-15 (NIV).

While it was a wise move to extricate Paul from the potential violence and harm, Silas and Timothy are now left to follow up with the new Berean church, those who had eagerly received Paul's message and were keen to find out more from the Old Testament Scriptures. Silas and Timothy regroup with Paul in Athens a little later. Later on in the trip we read that Paul, preparing to return to Jerusalem via Macedonia, sends *"two of his helpers, Timothy and Erasmus, to Macedonia..."* ahead of him. Acts 19:22 (NIV). Paul's confidence in Timothy is growing as no doubt is Timothy's ministry skills under Paul's influence. After regrouping, Paul decides to travel back through Macedonia as he was about to sail for Syria, due to his unpopularity with the Jews. In an interesting side note, Luke the author of Acts, notes, *"He was accompanied by Sopater son of Pyrrhus of Berea, Aristachus and Secundus from Thessalonica, Gaius from Derbe, Timothy also, and Tychicus and Trophinus from the province of Asia."* Acts 20:4 (NIV). He sends them ahead to Troas to wait for him there, perhaps as a decoy while he took a different route, eventually linking up again with them at Troas.

Paul appears to have selected people with great ministry potential and invited them into his travelling team, providing a mentoring umbrella for them to learn and develop their ministry skills. Along the way we see glimpses of him thrusting them out alone for ministry exercises, before returning to the team.

Priscilla and Aquila are another good example (Acts 18:2-3, 18-19). After Paul met this Jewish tent-maker married couple in Corinth and then stayed and worked with them, there is little doubt that they were among the converts in the emerging Corinthian church. After a year and a half of dedicated teaching in the new Corinthian church (Acts 18:11), and some additional time in Corinth, Paul departs for Ephesus enroute to Syria, with Priscilla and Aquila. He leaves them at Ephesus, no doubt confident that they could now be in a position to assist the growth of the new church there. After two years or more under Paul's mentorship, they are now ready to take on a pastoral ministry role themselves.

Timothy matured into a respected leader in the wider church, evidenced by the fact that a number of letters to the churches are written by Paul and Timothy, such as Colossians, Philippians and 2 Corinthians. Silas co-authored 1 & 2 Thessalonians with Paul and Timothy, and Sosthenes co-authored 1 Corinthians with Paul. Paul shares the limelight with his younger proteges, allowing their gifts to become exposed to the wider church.

The books of 1 & 2 Timothy are Paul's letters to Timothy. They contain not only advice on handling various situations he was encountering in the church, encouragements for his own spiritual and personal life, but very personal glimpses into their relationship, like a father and son. Paul refers to Timothy as *"my true son in the faith"*. 1 Timothy 1:2 (NIV), and *"my dear son"*. 2 Timothy 1:2 (NIV). In the first five verses of 2 Timothy 1, Paul pours out his heart at his remembrances of Timothy and the tears Timothy shed at their last departure. He speaks of the faith of his mother Eunice and grandmother Lois, which grounded Timothy's own faith. In the last verses of 2 Timothy 4, Paul urges Timothy to come and visit him under house arrest in Rome. *"Do your best to come to me quickly,"* he urges, *"Do your best to get here before winter." "When you come, bring the cloak that I left with Carpus at Troas, and my scrolls, especially the parchments."* 2 Timothy 4:9, 19, 13 (NIV). *"Stop drinking only water, and use a little wine because of your stomach and frequent illnesses,"* 1 Timothy 5:23 (NIV) shows Paul's concern for Timothy's welfare. The point is this, the strength of mentoring is the relationship, not just the transfer of information and skills.

)(

When a leader recognises potential in a team member, then a mentoring relationship may be the best way to provide a more personal and dedicated way to develop that potential. Some mentoring relationships may be very informal but the mentoree over time knows that at certain points in time the mentor has provided advice or encouragement, and is continuing to keep an eye on them. Others may be formal agreements where the mentor agrees to provide advice, skills training or encouragement with specific outcomes over a fixed time period. But in both cases the mentor has committed to a relationship based approach to developing the other persons' potential.

In our world of today, training has often become over formalised, based around attendance at a course and issuing of a certificate or diploma. What is learnt in a few days or weeks is quickly forgotten, often packed away in class notes to gather dust while the diploma hangs proudly on the office wall. We need to recognise that in fact the most valuable learning can occur in a much more informal mentoring relationship.

※

> In a Time magazine article some years ago, Nelson Mandela was asked about his leadership style. He replied that he learnt leadership when he was a small boy growing up in an African village herding cattle. He would walk behind the cattle with a small stick and if one started to stray, he would give it a light prod with the stick. That became his model of leadership.

Leading to Empower

QUESTIONS FOR DISCUSSION

1. How could you describe the relationship that Maria discovers Konio is providing? Is it a formal or informal relationship?

2. Can you identify anyone in your life who has had some sort of mentoring relationship with you, even if it is informal and not even described as mentoring? What did they do to encourage you or help build your skills or experience? Was it empowering for you?

3. In your work situation, can you identify a person who you could mentor in some way, perhaps with some life skill or work skill? Is there some skill that you have that you can help someone else learn informally through a mentoring relationship?

10. Values Driven Management

What drives a manager to succeed? There are many factors which provide motivation. It may be practical and self-centered, such as seeking to get a promotion or higher wage. It may be more obscure, driven by a fear of failing and perhaps losing the job. It may be driven by the practical need to complete a project by a certain date and so everything is focused on on-time delivery. It may be that the company's financial well-being is dependent on completing the current contract satisfactorily, so a longer term goal is driving the short term need.

If people matter more than projects, and relationships more than money, then to successfully implement strategies that demonstrate this, a company must be driven by core values which also express this. When people accept and start to live out these values, radical change happens.

While the Jewish nation was not a company as such, it was a community of people who God wanted to develop. Starting out as a rag-tag bunch of Hebrew slaves in Egypt, God sought to transform them into a nation that would influence the world. At the heart of this plan was an obedience to behaviour which was rooted in values.

At the heart of these values is a respect for each other, that is, people-centered values. The Ten Commandments enshrine these values with respect for God, life, marriage, property and relationships. The laws of Moses expanded in the books of Leviticus and Deuteronomy take these a step further, but at the heart is a blueprint for a society which honours God and respects others. Jesus only reinforced this when he declared in Mark 12:30-31 that loving God and loving your neighbour are the greatest commandments.

Let's consider one very important principle in the Old Testament, that of Jubilee. It comes out of the Sabbath principle, which is based on rest after a cycle of seven seasons. Most people are familiar with the Sabbath day, the seventh day when God rested from his work in Genesis 1. (See also Genesis 31:12-17). There is also a Sabbath year, the seventh year, and a Jubilee year, which is after 7 x 7 years - the 50th year. Various events and expectations for these years are advised in Leviticus 25 but they both expand on the period of rest extending to the land, servants and slaves, and even foreigners. I recommend reading Leviticus 25 before continuing to read this discussion about Jubilee.

When the land is returned to its original owners each 50 years, it guards against greedy real estate profiteers who would continue to escalate prices beyond the reach of the average person. The price of land reduces as each year edges closer to Jubilee year because the value of the land is in its useful years until Jubilee. God's abhorrence of one person ripping off or taking advantage of another is clear. This is a major problem in our societies today - real estate greed is at the heart of many social problems including squatter settlements and homelessness.

The creation of cities of refuge allowed for people to find a safe place if they had inadvertently committed an act requiring judicial involvement to determine their guilt. The value of natural justice inherent in this act again highlights the principle.

The instruction to care for the alien, foreigner, living among them as they would one of their own makes it clear that racism is not acceptable. People are equal in God's sight regardless of whether they are Jews or Gentile.

The provision for bond slaves to be released in the seventh year and given benefits to make sure they can manage their life in freedom demonstrates very practically this attitude of care for each other. The option to be accepted into a family should a slave wish to take on a lifetime of service, despite the pain of having a hole drilled in their ear, shows that for some slaves, service was a blessing and they became very much part of the family. Their children in some cases may even have married into the family.

Refugees, slaves, foreigners, all people who in many societies are seen as second class citizens, yet these are the ones whose rights are guaranteed in the law for God's people. The Old Testament Torah, the laws of Moses, are generally regarded as legalistic, rules to be obeyed or be judged. But at the heart of these laws is the value of respect for each other and the protection of even the most despised and vulnerable in society. You'll be surprised if you can start to read the OT not as a book of rules for which you will be judged, but as actions and behaviours which demonstrate the value of respect and care for each other, and of course honour and respect for God. The many very practical rules are an application of the values God upholds, designed to enable society to function as a healthy and vibrant community, practicing natural justice and love for each other.

Next time you read the Old Testament laws, ask the question, what value is this law demonstrating?

If we continue this thread into the New Testament we see Jesus' compassion for the prostitutes and tax collectors, thieves and Samaritans, the most despised people in the community. Even though he was a rabbi, a qualified teacher, revered for his teachings, wisdom, and authority, he chose simple men, fishermen, to become his main disciples. Women also became part of his extended group of outcasts. He held up children as having the simplest and most profound capacity for faith. He said that a Roman Centurion, a despised member of the Roman occupation military in Israel, had more faith than anyone in Israel that he had seen.

The arrogant religious leaders came under his constant criticism for their hypocrisy. The Saduccees were landowners and controlled the illegal market operation in the court of the Gentiles round the temple in Jerusalem where Jesus overturned the tables and caused a commotion to disrupt the trading. The Pharisees paraded around as if they were spiritual elites, closer to God than everyone else. But in reality they were empty shells and far away from God, enforcing laws without regard for people's situations, judging people as worthless in their poverty or misfortune. They had negated the word of God because they had missed the heart of what God wanted (Matthew 15:6-9) - not formal sacrifice and legalism but a heart for other people, to love mercy and act in kindness and walk humbly with God (Micah 6:8).

When laws are used to control people, the institution or organisation or even church becomes legalistic, dominated by bureaucracy and rules, and it loses its heart. People become fearful of breaking the law because of the punishment they may receive, whether that is seen as physical, emotional or spiritual. So they follow with their head, hands, feet and too often wallet, but not with their heart. They work to gain what they can. Job satisfaction and productivity decrease. People watch the clock and take every opportunity to use the company for their own advantage. They try to outsmart the system, seeing what they can get away with. Theft, corruption and self-interest start to dominate the culture of the organisation. Outsmarting the system becomes a value that drives people further down the path of self-interest.

But when good values drive an organisation, especially Biblically based values, and people embrace those values, it creates a climate of shared trust. Sacrifice, trust, care and compassion, selflessness, integrity, honesty and goodness become the norm. Those who don't want to follow those values find themselves on the outer. An attitude of respect creates a much more positive environment where people are encouraged to develop their own potential and that of their colleagues. Productivity increases as does staff morale and job satisfaction. It is empowering for people.

Values are set at Board and executive management level. Management must live out those values and demonstrate them to the workforce. A manager who is known to be stealing time or goods from his employer will only encourage those under him to do the same, even if he or she thinks no one notices it is happening. A manager who is forthright in standing up for good values and whose life demonstrates that integrity, will be a good advocate to encourage his or her staff to do the same.

Too often organisations expect employees just to follow the rules. But those that inspire their employees at all levels to be values driven and recognise that rules are there to enable the organisation's values to be applied, will find staff well-being and productivity greatly improved. Managers will find it easier to develop a deeper level of trust with their staff. Disciplinary action against staff members will be reduced and so staff morale and retention is improved.

QUESTIONS FOR DISCUSSION

1. If you were to write a list of values as a values statement for Jesus during his earthly ministry, what would you write?

2. Does your organisation have a statement of its values?

3. Can you write down at least 3 positive values that your organisation promotes?

4. If you were starting a company, what are five values that you consider are essential to any organisation?

5. In your management capacity, what practical steps can you take to move your team to be more positive values-centered? What is to stop you doing that now?

5. Write your own personal values statement, a list of one word values you consider important for your life.

6. Have you compromised your values in your work or in your private life? What can you do to be restored to good values again?

CASE STUDIES & SIMULATION EXERCISES

These case studies are best used for group discussion - read to the group and seek feedback on a response to the issue.

Simulation exercises (role plays) are best used by selecting two people to act out the roles, allowing them to see only their own role, with the rest of the group witnessing. Do not allow the group to know what the roles are so they can provide feedback from what they observe in the role plays. When the two participants have brought their act to a suitable conclusion, then halt it and call for feedback from the group. Sometimes actors will stumble and not actually resolve the problem. In that case, give them a clue as to how to continue but make sure they do come to a resolution. The leader may also throw in some additional information that changes the situation. Review the written roles at the end.

Case Studies - conflict resolution

1. It was a beautiful day with a fairly light program scheduled. As Base Manager, you (Bosi) were hoping for an easy day. You were proud of your team and the way they had worked well to improve standards at the base in the last 3 months. The number of pilot complaints had dropped significantly and so you knew things were improving.

After the first flight returned however, the pilot came to see you. He was clearly not happy.

"Bosi, what happened to the load this morning?" he said. He was definitely not happy!. "The aircraft seemed a bit heavy when I took off so I weighted the cargo after I landed.

I asked for 935kg and there was 1023kg actually on board. Are your staff trying to kill me? I'll have to report this but you better get your Traffic Officers doing a better job!"

You found the manifests and connotes and added up the total, but it came to 935kg. So it appears that extra cargo was loaded on the aircraft, but why and by whom? The Traffic Officer who signed the Manifest was one of your best Traffic Officers, Skelim Gut. He was a strong highlander, a very good worker but had been in the company for many years and was sometimes defensive about his work, and sometimes got into arguments too easily. You pulled him aside to speak with him about this.

"Hey Skelim, I've got a problem. The pilot reported that there was about 90kg more cargo on the aircraft than on the manifest and he was not very happy about it. You signed the manifest for the correct weight. Do you know what happened?" I asked him.

Immediately I could see that Skelim was starting to get upset with me now!

"I told that new Traffic Officer, you know, that pikinnini bilong nambis (coastal boy), that he was confusing the trolley loads and getting cargo mixed up. So why are you talking to me about it?" He lifted his hand and pointed his finger right in your face. " Couldn't you see that by hiring him you would have problems? I am tired of getting the blame all the time when things go wrong!" Skelim turned around and stormed away from me in anger.

You watch him walk away from you and then .....

How will you resolve this conflict?

Explain the steps you will use to find the route causes and then address them to resolve the conflict.

2. You are ready to approve a test drive for a client's very expensive car after major maintenance. As Workshop Supervisor, you (Girisi) are confident that your team of mechanics have performed well to get the car out 2 days earlier than planned. You are looking forward to a bbq this afternoon to thank the team.

During the routine post-maintenance—pre-test check, the Chief Mechanic notices something which concerns him. He calls you over and you both investigate further. It appears that a component fitted on the engine is not fitting quite right and that caught the CM's attention. He asks you why that part is fitted.

You decide to follow up with the mechanic who was working on the engine, Spana, and ask him about that part. He is one of your best mechanics but you know that his child has been quite sick and he has not been able to sleep well at night. He also confided in you that he and his wife have had some arguments recently.

"Yes I remember that," he says to you, in his normal calm manner. "I asked the stores person, Nambatu, about it when he gave it to me. He was a bit confused, probably because it was his first day back at work after having malaria, but he was absolutely certain that it was the correct part number. We looked at the tag together and then checked on the computer."

You then ask Spana if he had done a visual check of the new and old parts to make sure they were identical. Suddenly he turns to face you, and his face becomes angry.

"I'm tired of being blamed whenever things go wrong here," he yells at you. "Those stores boys don't know what they are doing and keep giving me wrong parts. Why do you have to pick on me, why don't you go and talk with them," he shouted as he pointed to Stores.

You take a deep breath and then ....

How will you resolve this conflict?

Explain the steps you will use to find the route causes and then address them to resolve the conflict.

Performance Management Simulations

SIM 1. You are the Admin Manager. You use a company vehicle one day and discover a betel nut husk on the floor. Recently another employee advised that Jedy, one of your administration staff (who you know does not chew betel nut), had been seen at the market buying vegetables and getting into the vehicle with several people who were not company staff. You decide that you will raise this issue with Jedy at the next performance management meeting, and schedule the meeting. Jedy has entered your office and so you now speak with her.

SIM 1. Jedy - Several months ago you were using a company vehicle for company business when your aunty flagged you down in the street and asked you to take her to a shop. You advised her that you cannot do that but she insisted, and so you thought you could do it just this once. However, soon after, the same thing happened again, but she wanted to go to the market. So this started to happen regularly - every Wednesday you would get the vehicle under the pretext of a work run but use it to take your aunty to the market. You know your aunty and her friends who were now joining her were betel nut chewers but you asked them not to chew in the vehicle. The situation had caused you much stress and in fact you could never sleep well on Tuesday night because you were afraid you would be found out, but the pressure from your aunty was too strong. The Admin Manager, your supervisor, has just called you and asked to see you for a performance counselling session and you are now very afraid you have been found out and will lose your job.

SIM 2. You notice one of your field officers is not wearing PPE on the tarmac while loading a plane. As an Operations Supervisor you need to address this with him. However you immediately instruct him to stay off the tarmac area until he has PPE. He is not happy with you. So you meet with him to find out the facts and find a resolution.

SIM 2. Field Officer. Your hi-vis vest got ripped when loading a mower yesterday and is unserviceable. However there are no spares at the base, and when you went to stores, they had none in stock. You decided to continue to work even though you did not have a vest because you love your work at the airport and want to continue to serve the community. You know that it would let the team down also if you could not work. So you are unhappy that you have been taken off the tarmac when none of the situation is your responsibility.

Leading to Empower

SIM 3. You are a Shift Supervisor working with a team preparing manufactured goods for dispatch by truck. You have observed one of your team members has often disappeared during the day for an hour or more. Whenever you have asked them about it, they have replied that they needed to go to the toilet, or had a headache and needed to rest. You suspect that this is a sign of some problems they are having in the workplace. During the next performance management meeting with them, you try to find out what the real problem is, and how you can help the staff member to perform better. He enters your office now.

SIM 3. Dispatcher - You are called on for a performance review meeting with your Supervisor. You have been struggling with some things but have not wanted to tell the Supervisor about them in case you are disciplined or even lose your job. Several weeks ago you injured your foot when a piece of equipment dropped off the cargo trolley onto your toes while preparing to load it on the truck. Then you also cut your hand when loading some loose objects which were sharp. The company supplied gloves but they are worn out with holes in the fingers, and you have not received the steel cap boots promised. You don't feel that you can be committed to the organisation when they are not meeting their obligations to issue PPE and make sure it is in good condition.

Leading to Empower

SIM 4 Program Manager: You have been monitoring a field supervisor who has been preparing for a field trip. You are expecting that he will have all equipment prepared to go 4 days before departure date so are surprised when he comes in 2 days before departure and wants to delay the departure and reschedule the flights by 2 days. He advises you that he has not been able to get everything ready in time. You call him in for a performance management meeting to discover why this performance gap has happened and how it can be avoided in future.

SIM 4 Field Supervisor: You are a Field Supervisor preparing for a field trip. One of your staff has been having some problems at home and has skipped work for a few days while he sorts it out. This has put extra work load on you at what is already a busy time. You have had to take on his workload. You don't mind because you love to do more and make sure the job is done properly. With 2 days to go before the team departs, you realise you have not assembled all the equipment and so find you need to stay back till 10pm at night to sort it out. However in the end you have to reschedule the program and delay the flight by 2 days. When you advise your Project Manager, he advises that you need to have a talk about it and he calls you into his office for a performance management meeting.

Leading to Empower

About the Author

Michael Jelliffe is an Australian who has worked in a number of management roles in both Australia and Papua New Guinea in his career spanning nearly 50 years. Working in aviation and church based organisations, roles have included operational, safety and executive management as well as flying and training. He has also served as a Director on the Board of a number of church-based, governmental and commercial organisations.

His passion is teaching in cross cultural environments, especially Biblical truths, and helping people discover their God given potential. This book has been written from material he has developed conducting frontline management training courses and from his own management experience.

As well as aviation qualifications, he holds an MA in Intercultural Studies and certification in Quality Auditing and Training. He is a member of the PNG Institute of Directors and a Pastor of the Evangelical Church of PNG.

For feedback to the author, or to order this book, email to nengebooks1@gmail.com

www.ingramcontent.com/pod-product-compliance
Lightning Source LLC
Chambersburg PA
CBHW050320010526
44107CB00055B/2320